EARLY HISTORY

OF

CARTER COUNTY

1760-1861

By
Frank Merritt
Elizabethton, Tennessee

East Tennessee Historical Society
Knoxville, Tennessee

Copyright 1950
Frank Merritt

All rights reserved. No part of this publication may be reproduced, stored in a retrieval system or transmitted in any form or by any means without the prior written permission of the publisher.

Please direct all correspondence and orders to:

SOUTHERN HISTORICAL PRESS, Inc.
PO BOX 1267
375 West Broad Street
Greenville, SC 29601
southernhistoricalpress@gmail.com

ISBN #0-89308-904-4

Dedicated to
ROSALIE
and
Little CARL and ELAINE
Who Have Sacrificed Most

PREFACE

Recent surveys have indicated that people as a whole do not know too much concerning the history of our nation. Unfortunately, this is all the more true of most of the people in many of the counties of Tennessee with respect to their own local history. Therefore, my primary purpose in this study has been to inform myself of the history of Carter County and secondly to do my part in helping to preserve for our children and future generations something of this interesting past. Since the writer is a native of Carter County and a descendant of some of those early pioneers, this research project has been conducted as a labor of love and respect to those who have handed down to us such a rich and treasured heritage.

This study has been limited to four aspects of the early county history, namely, government and politics, religious development, educational development, and slavery and secession. It is fully realized that other aspects of the county history such as industries, agriculture, transportation and families might have been selected and would have proved just as fruitful in the findings. It is earnestly hoped that further research will develop these and other aspects of the county history. An introductory chapter, briefly surveying the activities in the Watauga country prior to 1796, has been added to furnish the necessary background for the study.

Courtesy demands that acknowledgment should be made when help and encouragement have been given. My thanks are extended to Mr. Frank Percy, County Court Clerk, Mr. Ernest C. Buckles, Register of Deeds, Mrs. W. M. Vaught, Mr. and Mrs. J. Frank Seiler, Mrs. L. W. McCown, Mrs. B. D. Akard, Mr. Fred Hinkle, Mr. William Jenkins, the Rev. Edward M. Umbach, formerly minister of the First Presbyterian Church in Elizabethton, the Rev. E. H. Ogle, minister of the First Methodist Church in Elizabethton, Miss Pollyanna Creekmore of Lawson McGhee Library, Knoxville, and Mr. Robert Quarles of the State Archives in Nashville. Assistance was also given by personnel of the libraries of the State of Tennessee, University of Tennessee, and East Tennessee State College. Two close friends, Mr. Robert T. Nave, now a colleague at Hampton High School, and Miss Hildred Wagner, my "favorite" teacher and former colleague at Elizabethton High School, have been closely connected with the undertaking. Without their help the writer would have been greatly handicapped. Certain students in the writer's American history classes at the Elizabethton High School from 1948 to 1950 assisted in gathering pertinent data. Recognition is made of Dr. LeRoy P. Graf and Dr. Harold S. Fink of the History Department of the University of Tennessee who carefully read the manuscript and made valuable suggestions. My personal thanks and deep appreciation are extended to Dr. Stanley J. Folmsbee of the History Department of the University of Tennessee under whose direction this study was begun and completed. His suggestions and interest in the work have been at all times both helpful and inspirational.

This work as an original Master's thesis was submitted in August, 1950 to the Graduate School of the University of Tennessee. Their cooperation and assistance given by personal friends and the East Tennessee Historical Society make possible its publication.

Valley Forge
Elizabethton, Tennessee

Frank Merritt

TABLE OF CONTENTS

| CHAPTER | PAGE |

I. THE WATAUGA COUNTRY FROM 1760 TO 1796 1

The long-hunters and Indian traders, James Robertson and his party of settlers, why settlers came, Watauga association of 1772, more early settlers, Transylvania Purchase at Sycamore Shoals, creation of Washington County, Indian attack on Watauga, Battle of King's Mountain, the Franklin Movement, the Watauga country under the Southwest Territorial Government, and admission of Tennessee into the Union.

II. GOVERNMENT AND POLITICS 30

Creation and organization of Carter County, location of the county seat, early tax rates and the county court, building the second and third courthouses, the movement to change the county seat, creation and establishment of Johnson County, changes in county as result of 1834 constitution, division of the county into civil districts, disputes over the incorporation of Elizabethton, county's first newspapers, Brownlow and the Elizabethton Whig, county votes against Jackson, Whig influence in Carter County, reasons why county voted Whig, description of the 1844 election in the county, Whig vote appears under the American and Constitutional-Union parties later.

III. RELIGIOUS GROWTH OF CARTER COUNTY 71

Influence of Regulators, claims of Sinking Creek Baptist Church, why the Sinking Creek story has been confused, spread of Sinking Creek's influence to Stoney Creek and Doe River Cove, congregation split over Fanny Renfro's baptism, preachers that have gone out from Sinking Creek, reasons why members were "disfellowshipped," church helped to settle civil disputes, early membership, Stoney Creek Baptist Church, interest in missionary efforts, membership, Watauga Baptist Church, revivals and membership, Zion Baptist Church on Gap Creek, Laurel Fork Baptist Church, Elizabethton Baptist Church, its early officials and ministers, Turkeytown as an "arm of the church," efforts to build a house of worship, cooperation with other churches, missionary-mindedness, membership, earliest activities of the Methodists, John Singletary as founder of Elizabethton Methodists, erection of first church building, Elizabethton circuit, Brownlow as circuit rider, revivals and camp meetings as seen in the Whig, the Elizabethton circuit in 1843, Watauga and Taylorsville circuits created, N. G. Taylor as preacher, leadership in the temperance movement, early membership, Presbyterians and Rev. Samuel Doak, influence of nearby Presbyterian schools, organization of Elizabethton Presbyterian Church, early officials and ministers, temperance resolution, construction of church building, finances of the church, early membership, Buffalo Creek and the Christian Churches, early treasurer's report, Turkeytown Christian Church, Mt. Pleasant Christian Church.

CHAPTER	PAGE
IV. EDUCATIONAL DEVELOPMENT IN CARTER COUNTY	124

Children of wealthiest families sent away to school, chartering of Duffield Academy in 1806, old building used also as church, 1848 Academy Report, the academy affairs as seen in the Whig, purposes of the academy, Elizabethton Female Academy as seen in the Whig, how was the female school financed?, the Emma Female Academy, the "binding out" of orphans and others to secure practical occupational training, the apprenticeship system, "pauper school" stigma attached to common schools, the law of 1830 concerning common schools, pupil population and methods of financing the common schools, first women teachers, wages of teachers, location of some early schools.

V. SLAVERY AND SECESSION IN CARTER COUNTY 149

Slavery during the Watauga Association, slavery during the period before statehood, slavery from the 1797 tax list, slavery and the tax rate, observations concerning the sale and transfer concerning slaves in the county, emancipation by legal actions, treatment accorded the slave in Carter County differs from the popular opinion, the Negro admitted to church membership, the congressional election of 1859, 1860 presidential election, the first Tennessee vote on secession, East Tennessee Convention against secession, Tennessee votes to secede, division of opinion in Carter County, remains largely Union in sentiment.

VI. SUMMARY. 170

BIBLIOGRAPHY 173

APPENDIX 179

Population of Carter County (1791-1860), Some Original Grantees to Land in Carter County, Officers of Carter County, Chairmen of the County Court (1836-1860), List of Early Magistrates in Carter County Showing Date of Appointment, etc., List of First Civil Districts and Names of First Magistrates Elected by People (1836), Known District Polling Places after 1836, Members of the County Court (1842-1860), Pastors and Clerks of the Sinking Creek Baptist Church, Pastors of the Stoney Creek Baptist Church, Charter Members of the Elizabethton Baptist Church, Early Methodist Circuit Riders, Charter Members of the First Presbyterian Church, Early Members of the Buffalo Creek Christian Church, Biographical Sketch of George Duffield, Officers, Teachers and Students of Duffield Academy, District Common School Commissioners Elected by the People (1838), Comparison of Scholastic Population (Common Schools), Common Schools, Their Location and Patrons, Negroes, Slave and Free, in Carter County.

CHAPTER ONE

THE WATAUGA COUNTRY FROM 1760 TO 1796

The Land of the Wataugans--how filled with implied descriptions and historical memories is this phrase! How blest are the people who dwell in the region encircled by majestic mountains and natural scenery as beautiful as ever met mortal eyes. Before the coming of the white settlers how loved the region must have been by the Indian warrior and his maid, for it was here that they cleared lands and fields and tilled some of its rich fertile soil. How thrilled must have been the hearts of the first "Long Hunters" and early settlers as they looked down from the crest of the mountains to the transmontane region of some cleared fields, bountiful springs of crystal cool mountain waters, forests of virgin timbers, and a sure supply of wild meats from the same forests. To them it must have seemed a "Promised Land."

Little wonder is there that from the picturesque banks of the beautiful Watauga and Doe Rivers were developed the Watauga Settlements, the early cradle of civilization in Tennessee. Numerous have been the great leaders who developed to maturity in this region or who spent their formative years within this realm.

It was only natural, then, that the early settlers would develop our country's first free government west of the Blue Ridge Mountains. These free men would risk their all in defense of this new-found liberty to help their neighbors retain lands and property against Indian raids. They could also be expected to assist the Revolutionary cause against the oppressive rule of George III symbolized by Major Patrick Ferguson and his army of Tories perched on top of King's Mountain. Such was the land and such were the people who first settled and inhabited the area now known as Carter County.

Earliest Settlements

The long-hunters and early Indian traders were perhaps the first whites to see the county. It is impossible to say who might have been the first to see the land, but it is known that Daniel Boone made his way through what is now the city of Elizabethton. Only a few miles from the county line is located Boone's Creek where the famous hunter carved his name and recorded the fact that he killed a bear in the year 1760.[1] Tradition handed down through the years relates that Boone "had a camp at a bold spring near the base of Buffalo Mountain."[2] It seems reasonable to assume, therefore, that Boone saw much of the present county and that he carried the news concerning the fine lands back to his friends and relatives in the Yadkin River country.

---

[1] To have reached Boone's Creek from the Yadkin River he must have come through Boone, North Carolina, on through the mountain gap between Zionsville on the Carolina side and Trade, Tennessee, on the Watauga River and down the stream past present Elizabethton. Two markers have been placed, one on the Harold McCormick School campus and the other just across the street on the Grace Baptist Church lawn, showing the route Boone probably followed.

[2] Samuel C. Williams, Dawn of Tennessee Valley and Tennessee History (Johnson City: The Watauga Press, 1937), 319. Hereafter cited, Williams, Dawn.

Concerning the earliest Indian traders, one writer dates their arrival "perhaps 1766" when Andrew Greer and Julius Caesar Dugger were trading in the Watauga country.³ It is quite likely that they erected a cabin somewhere along the Watauga and for the next three or four years made frequent trips between their original homes in Virginia and the Cherokee towns, carrying furs and pelts one way and merchandise and trinkets back for the furtherance of their trading.

One settler can definitely be identified, and it is certain that he lived in what later became Carter County. When James Robertson crossed the mountains from Orange County, North Carolina (which later became famous as the scene of the Alamance battle with the "Regulators"), during the spring of 1770, he accepted the hospitality of a hunter named John Honeycut who probably had also wandered over the mountains and who, because he liked the place, had just decided to remain and build for himself a small cabin on the banks of one of the tributaries of the Watauga.⁴ It was just where Doe River joins the Watauga, the present site of Elizabethton, that Robertson planted a crop of corn in fields that later became known as the Watauga Old Fields, meaning that

---

³J. G. M. Ramsey, The Annals of Tennessee to the End of the Eighteenth Century (Philadelphia: Lippincott, Grambo & Company, 1853), 142. Herafter cited, Ramsey, Annals.

⁴Ibid., 104; Williams, Dawn, 340; A. V. Goodpasture, "The Watauga Association," American Historical Magazine, III, No. 2 (April 1898), 108-110.

the Indians had used them and cleared them.[5] When his corn had been "laid by," Robertson began his return journey, and after more than usual trials in the mountains he reached his family.

Before his first visit to the Watauga country in search of a home which would be more distant from British control, Robertson was asked by some of his friends to locate suitable sites near his own for them. In the spring of 1771, therefore, Robertson and his family and friends made up "a party of sixteen" and "headed westward for the Watauga Valley."[6] James Robertson thus became "the leading spirit of the Watauga settlements where he proved himself in every way worthy of the affectionate title later conferred upon him after his activities in settling Middle Tennessee--"Father of Tennessee."[7]

By 1771 or earlier a trickle of settlers had begun to migrate from the western valley of southwest Virginia. In a few years it is probably true that more Virginians were present in the Watauga region than settlers who had migrated across the mountains from North Carolina.

---

[5] The Watauga Old Fields in the larger sense "extended from the mouth of Stoney Creek down the river to the mouth of Buffalo Creek at the bend of the river, about eight miles. And wherever there was a level or bottom piece of land along any river or creek in Carter County, there was an old field or deserted /Indian/ village." N. E. Hyder, "Watauga Old Fields," *American Historical Magazine*, VIII, No. 2 (July 1903), 253.

[6] Williams, Dawn, 342. He lists as members of the party James' brothers, Charles, Mark, and Jonathan, as well as his brother-in-law, William Reeves. Charles Robertson took up land on Sinking Creek.

[7] Goodpasture, loc. cit., 110.

The older writers like Ramsey believed that North Carolina "sent forth most of the emigrants to Watauga," but the more recent school of thought, led by Judge Samuel C. Williams, disagrees with Ramsey and contends the "on the Watauga the Virginian element was the largest."[8] Abernethy seems to settle the question in favor of Virginia when he considers the influence of the topography. "If geography counts anything in the migrations of peoples, if they follow valleys, rather than cross mountains, this must have been the case."[9] Further evidence of this point might be adduced by the fact that in 1772 the settlers, thinking themselves in Virginia territory, adopted Virginia laws and first appealed to the Old Dominion State in 1776 when threatened by the Cherokees.

It is of passing interest to note why the early settlers braved the dangers of life in the new country. Why did they leave behind friends and such comforts as they had in their earlier homes? Most of the early settlers had come westward "to improve their conditions, by subduing and cultivating the new lands." They had been "prompted

---

[8] Ramsey, Annals, 103; Samuel C. Williams, Tennessee During the Revolutionary War (Nashville: The Tennessee Historical Commission, 1944), 2. Hereafter cited, Williams, Revolutionary War. Williams (p. 1) estimated that 75% of the settlers had migrated directly from Virginia and that another 5% were of Virginia birth.

[9] Thomas P. Abernethy, From Frontier to Plantation in Tennessee (Chapel Hill: The University of North Carolina Press, 1932), 9.

by the noble ambition of forming a new community, of laying broad and deep the foundation of government, and of acquiring, under it, distinction and consequence for themselves and their children." Others, probably inspired by these same motives, were also seeking a refuge from the misgovernment of the seaboard colonies of which they were a part, as was the case of the Carolina Regulators. Still others came seeking refuge from "justice in their own country," hoping to escape the demands of the law and punishment for their crimes by a "retreat to these remote and inaccessible frontiers."[10] However, this latter group was soon recognized for what it was; swift justice, as well as life, on the frontier was rough and crude.[11]

The Watauga Association

Late in 1771 John Donelson and Alexander Cameron, Indian agents among the Cherokees for the English, and a group of the Cherokee leaders marked the boundary between the whites and the Indians. Much to the disappointment of the Wataugans they learned they were not in Virginia, as previously supposed, but were in North Carolina and on lands which belonged to the Indians. Cameron advised the

---

[10] Ramsey, Annals, 103-106.

[11] Many were run out of the country—"they'll soon take poplar and push off" - a poplar canoe as means of leaving the country. Williams, Dawn, 354; and story related to the writer by "Uncle" Grant Ellis, son of Captain Dan Ellis of Civil War fame, in interview, September, 1949.

Wataugans to move at once, but they always gave one excuse or another, stalling for more time.

In 1772 these early settlers found themselves in a unique position--far out on the frontier beyond the pale of Virginia government, and encroaching on the Indian lands within the charter bounds of the colony of North Carolina. At that time there were about "seventy plantations" in the settlement and probably as many heads of families.[12] These freemen came together and formed a frontier system of government for the management of affairs of common interest. Thus these pioneers exercised the "divine right of governing themselves," and formed "the first written compact for civil government anywhere west of the Alleghanies."[13] Five officers or commissioners were appointed and the majority of them were to settle all matters in dispute. One writer has described the form of government set up under the famous Articles of Watauga Association of 1772 as "paternal and patriarchal--simple and moderate, but summary and firm."[14]

---

[12] Williams, Dawn, 364.

[13] Ramsey, Annals, 107. Another historian has said of the Watauga Association: "They formed a written constitution, the first ever adopted west of the mountains, or by a community composed of American-born freemen. . . . The Watauga settlers outlined in advance the nation's work. They tamed the rugged and shaggy wilderness, they bid defiance to outside foes, and they successfully solved the problem of self-government. . . . The bulk of the settlers were men of sterling worth; fit to be the pioneer fathers of a mighty and beautiful state." Theodore Roosevelt, Winning of the West, 6 Vols. (New York: G. P. Putnam's Sons, 1889, I), 216, 227.

[14] Ramsey, Annals, 107.

The original document of the Articles of the Watauga Association has been lost, but from contemporary sources something can be learned of its workings, the reasons why it was formed, and other details. Later the Wataugans in their petition for assistance to North Carolina stated the reason for this government in the following terms:

> Finding ourselves on the Frontiers, and being apprehensive that, for want of a legislature, we might become a shelter for such as endeavored to defraud their creditors; considering also the necessity of recording Deeds, Wills, and doing other public business, we, by the consent of the people, formed a court for the purposes above mentioned taking (by desire of our constitutents) the Virginia laws for our guide, so near as the situation of affairs would admit; this was intended for ourselves, and was done by the consent of every individual.[15]

This five man court (or commission) was composed of John Carter, probably chairman of the group, assisted by James Robertson, Charles Robertson, cousin to James, Zachariah Isbell, and a fifth not certainly known.[16]

Having satisfactorily solved the problem of government, the settlers then made certain their tenure of lands whereon they resided. In their account of activities to the Provincial Council of North

---

[15] Ibid., pp. 134-138; Williams, Dawn, pp. 368-372.

[16] Ramsey named John Sevier the fifth member and clerk, but Williams doubted this inasmuch as Sevier did not settle in the Watauga country until 1775, having lived in the North-of-Holston since 1773. Williams believed that the fifth member might have been Jacob Brown. Dawn, pp. 373-375.

Carolina in 1776 the settlers related that

> . . . being too inconveniently situated to move back, and feeling an unwillingness to loose the labour bestowed on their plantations, they applied to the Cherokee Indians, and leased the land for a term of ten years.[17]

Negotiating the lease for the Wataugans were James Robertson and John Boon (Boone) who bargained, obtaining the lease in return "for an amount of merchandise, estimated to be worth five or six thousand dollars, some muskets, and other articles of convenience."[18]

For some three or four years this system of government worked well and the settlement continued to grow. Under the leadership of John Carter, the Robertsons, and others, a period of prosperity resulted. However, it was not long until the royal governor of Virginia, the Earl of Dunmore, took notice of the happenings and in a letter to Lord Dartmouth lamented the state of affairs in the back country:

> We have an example of the very case, there being actually a set of people on the back part of this colony, bordering on the Cherokee country, who, finding they could not obtain titles to the land they fancied under any of the neighboring governments, have settled upon it without, and contented themselves by becoming in a manner tributary to the Indians, and have appointed magistrates, and framed laws for their present occasion; and, to all intents and purposes, erected themselves into, though an inconsiderable, yet a separate State. It at least sets a dangerous example to the people of America forming governments distinct from and independent of his Majesty's authority.[19]

---

[17] Williams, Revolutionary War, 19; Ramsey, Annals, 135.

[18] Ibid., 109. Unfortunately Ramsey is not consistent on this point. Following Haywood's earlier account, he said "for eight years," but later quotes the entire petition, which he himself found, and therein the words "for a term of ten years" are used.

[19] Williams, Dawn, 371.

During the peaceful years between 1771 and 1774, and especially after the lease of lands from the Indians by the Wataugans, settlement of the area progressed at a quickened pace. Along the bottom lands of the Watauga and Doe Rivers and the many tributary creeks, rude log cabins were constructed and larger clearings were made. The Robertsons and their group were soon joined by Valentine and John Sevier, Michael Hyder, James Edens, Teeter Nave, Thomas and Joshua Houghton, Henry Lyle, Leonard Hart, Joshua Williams, Andrew Taylor, and John Carter.[20] These and others who joined them became the ancestors and progenitors of many of the familes that largely people the county today. Many of their descendants have migrated, however, and have settled in all parts of the southwest and farther west, many of them having become very prominent in their new locations.

The Transylvania Purchase

Sycamore Shoals (about a mile and one-half below Elizabethton) was the scene of some important negotiations with the Cherokees. During March of 1775 "a thousand or twelve hundred Cherokees ... about half

---

[20]Ibid., pp. 430-438; Ramsey, Annals, pp. 141-142; Williams, Revolutionary War, pp. 22-23, lists the names of the Wataugans who signed the petition sent to North Carolina asking for protection. In the appendix (p. 181) the reader will find a more extended list of early settlers and the immediate location of their claims as found by the writer after studies of deeds and land grants in the offices of the Registers of Deeds in Elizabethton and Jonesboro.

of whom were men,"[21] headed by such important chiefs as the Little Carpenter, Dragging Canoe, and the Raven, met with Judge Richard Henderson, the chief promoter, and other members of the Transylvania Company, organized in North Carolina. For "ten thousand pounds sterling, in money and in goods,"[22] the Indians sold to Henderson and Company on March 17, 1775, "some twenty million acres, including almost all of the present state of Kentucky and an immense tract in Tennessee, comprising all the territory watered by the Cumberland River and all its tributaries." It was during this discussion with the Indians that one of their leaders, Dragging Canoe, in an impassioned address warned the whites, dramatically pointing toward the west, that "a Dark Cloud hung over that land, which was known as the Bloody Ground."[23]

The Wataugans profited by the gathering of so large a number because Henderson and Company bought food, chiefly beeves and cornmeal, from the settlers.[24] This ready market probably enabled the

---

[21] William S. Lester, The Transylvania Colony (Spencer, Indiana: Samuel R. Guard & Co., 1935), p. 32. Chapter II gives a good account of the Sycamore Shoals or Watauga Treaty with the Indians.

[22] Archibald Henderson, The Conquest of the Old Southwest (New York: The Century Company, 1920), pp. 224, 225. Although Henderson and Lester disagree as to the motives and methods used by Judge Henderson, they are in substantial agreement as to the negotiations with the Indians. Lester claims there was no treaty made at all, merely "a deed from the Cherokees to the members of Henderson and Company." Lester, op. cit., p. 36.

[23] Henderson, op. cit., p. 224.

[24] Williams, Dawn, p. 405. He referred to the transaction as "the most colossal ... by individuals or a private corporation that America has ever seen."

inhabitants of the area to make their own purchase of lands from the Indians on March 19, 1775, when Charles Robertson acting on behalf of the Watauga Association bought "for two thousand pounds" the lands that had earlier been leased.[25] A land office was immediately opened by the Watauga ns with James Smith as clerk and William Bailey Smith as surveyor. Patents and grants were then issued to all those holding pre-emption rights, and thus the earliest land grants in Carter County were legalized.[26] Lands were also available for sale to newcomers.

Petition and Attack

Sometime after George Washington was appointed Commander-in-Chief of the American armies, the settlers of the Watauga country decided to name their section "Washington District," thus giving to this country the honor of being the first territorial and geographical division named in honor of the great Revolutionary leader.[27] Feeling

---

[25] Henderson, op. cit., p. 224. About this same time Henderson bought a narrow strip connecting his Transylvania purchase with the Watauga-Holston settlements because he "did not love to walk on their /Indian/ lands" and gave in return for this additional land "some Goods, Guns and Ammunition" which the Indians had not yet seen. Jacob Brown purchased the lands whereon the Nolichucky settlements had been made.

[26] Williams, Dawn, pp. 414-415. Perhaps the earliest patent was issued to Joshua Houghton for "a tract of land lying on the south side of Wataugah /sic./ half a mile below the mouth of Doe River." This land was later acquired by Samuel Tipton and is at present the home of the famous "Bemberg" rayon.

[27] Samuel C. Williams, "The First Territorial Division Named for Washington," Tennessee Historical Magazine, Series II, Vol. II, (April, 1932), pp. 153-169.

that the Indians would soon be upon them and their families, the inhabitants in the early spring of 1776 called upon Virginia for assistance to meet the expected attacks. Apparently they were not encouraged by the Virginia legislature,[28] for in July in the lengthy petition of 1776 already mentioned they informed the North Carolina legislature of all their actions and intentions. They urged that there should be no delay "in annexing us to your Province, in such a manner as your wisdom shall direct." The petition cited their willingness to participate in and lend assistance to the Revolutionary cause. They pledged "that nothing will be lacking or anything neglected, that may add weight (in the civil or military establishments) to the glorious cause in which we are struggling, or contribute to the welfare of our own or ages yet to come."[29]

Earlier the Watauga Association had put itself on an emergency footing, having chosen by unanimous consent a committee of safety as was the practice throughout the colonies. John Carter was elected

---

[28] Williams, Revolutionary War, p. 18.

[29] Ibid., p. 22. The entire petition with the names of the 114 signers is quoted by Williams, pp. 19-23. It is noteworthy that only two of the freemen could not write their names -- a good indication of the early education of the first settlers. Unfortunately this ratio of literacy was not maintained in the later years.

chairman, and it was this committee[30] that sought aid from Virginia and North Carolina and corresponded with Henry Stuart and Alexander Cameron, British agents among the Indians in the South. These agents warned the settlers that unless they vacated these outpost settlements immediately they could expect attacks by the Indians. By a series of letters exchanged between Carter and the agents the settlers were given a few extra days in which to make ready their defenses, but this merely postponed the attack for a while.[31]

The Indian attack on the Wataugans occurred on July 21, 1776, at their fortified location, sometimes referred to as Fort Caswell and sometimes as Fort Watauga, which was probably located near the Sycamore Shoals. The redmen under Chief Old Abram beseiged the fort

---

[30] In addition to John Carter as chairman, the committee consisted of Charles and James Robertson, Zachariah Isbell, John Sevier, James Smith, Jacob Brown, William Bean, John Jones, George Russell, Jacob Womack, Robert Lucas, and Felix Walker who served as clerk. Walker soon went on an expedition to assist the Americans at Charleston and was replaced by William Tatham, an Englishman, but a very good friend of John Carter. Unfortunately the marker on the Carter County courthouse lawn confuses this committee of safety (sometimes also referred to as the committee of thirteen) with the earlier committee or court of five under the Watauga Association.

[31] Philip H. Hamer, Tennessee A History 1673-1932, 4 Vols., (New York: The American Historical Society, 1935), I, pp. 73-88. Unlike most historians Hamer does not attribute the attack on white settlements to British intrigues among the Indians, but rather to constant encroachments of whites upon lands which the young warriors claimed as their own, not open to white settlement, and certain other reasons.

for several days, but finally dispersed when defeat of those within the fort seemed impossible. The fort was under the command of Colonel John Carter, assisted by Captain James Robertson, and Lieutenant John Sevier. The defending force, according to Tatham, a participant, numbered seventy-five.[32] A force of rangers sent out by Captain Evan Shelby, Jr., from the North-of-Holston settlements came to the assistance of the Wataugans but arrived too late to be of much help; they did, however, proceed to the Nolichucky region and proved an effective barrier to further Indian raids. Later Colonel William Christian's expedition from southwest Virginia, aided by some North Carolina troops, carried the war into the Cherokee towns and forced the Indians to ask for peace.

---

[32]Williams, Revolutionary War, pp. 44-47. It was at the battle of Fort Caswell that the young Catherine (Bonny Kate) Sherrill was rescued from certain death when she outran the savages and was given a saving hand by John Sevier who later married her. Another dramatic incident was the forethought of Ann Robertson who, seeing the Indians trying to scale the fort's walls, dashed boiling water from the washday pots upon their bare skin. Though wounded, she must have achieved a howling success! Ibid.

Washington District

When North Carolina established her own state government after getting rid of the royal governor and his assistants, then she turned her attention to the settlers in the back country. Acceding to their petition of 1776, she organized the Washington District into a county named "Washington County," establishing the court early in 1777. Colonel John Carter became chairman of the court and also entry-taker for the new county.[33] Settlers reinforced their land titles from James Robertson and the purchase from the Indians by having these titles confirmed by the North Carolina government.[34] Carter was also the first senator from across the mountains while John Sevier and Jacob Womack were the members in the general assembly. Later in 1779 Jonesborough was laid out as the first county seat of Washington County in honor of Willie Jones, early friend of the over-mountain people. Jonesborough thus became the first town established in the state. In the same year the section of Washington County lying north of the Holston River was created into a new county to honor General John Sullivan of the continental army.[35]

---

[33] Ibid., 75-80. Other court members who are known to have lived in what later became Carter County included Andrew Greer, John McNabb, Thomas Houghton, and Charles Robertson.

[34] Settlers were not required to pay for lands until January, 1779. The rate was fifty shillings per one hundred acres. The head of the family was allowed 640 acres and he could enter 100 acres for his wife and each member of his family. Any acreage above this would cost five pounds per 100 acres. Abernethy, op. cit., 35.

[35] Williams, Revolutionary War, 123-127.

King's Mountain

For the over-mountain men the year of 1780 was a challenge, and King's Mountain, the turning point of the Revolutionary War in the South, was the command performance. Major Patrick Ferguson, threatening to carry the war into their own lands, sent a message to Colonel Evan Shelby warning him and the other Revolutionary sympathizers that if they "did not desist from their opposition to the British arms, he would march his army over the mountains, hang their leaders and lay waste their country with fire and sword."[36] Immediately Shelby and Sevier swung into operation. They agreed to invite Colonel William Campbell of Washington County, Virginia, to participate in the planned campaign.

During the time preceding the rendezvous at Sycamore Shoals on the Watauga, the people of the community were very busy. From the Matthew Talbot mill came meal for breadmaking; on Powder Branch a young woman named Mary Patton, according to tradition, was engaged in making powder to assist the soldiers. Beeves were being rounded up for meat supply; breads were being baked; clothes and rough uniforms were mended.

September 25 was fixed as the date of the rendezvous on the property of Pharoah Cobb, plantation and slave owner. Ready for the

---

[36] Ibid., 141, citing the Draper Manuscripts, Wisconsin Historical Society, Madison. All writers on this phase of American history are greatly indebted to this famous collection of papers relating to the King's Mountain story and the settlement of the whole of the old Southwest.

march were some 240 men under Sevier, a similar number under Shelby, and about 400 under Campbell. Added to these were several refuges from over the mountain under Colonel Charles McDowell. After a brief religious service conducted by the Rev. Samuel Doak in which he bade them Godspeed, they advanced up Gap Creek, crossed Doe River, camped the first night at Shelving Rock, about a mile above Roan Mountain. On the next day it was thought best to turn the cattle back. After killing some for meat supplies, the commands went forward and spent the second night on the bald of the Roan where the snow was "shoe-mouth deep."[37]

The expedition was imperiled on the second day when two men from Nolichucky under Sevier were discovered as missing. Later over-mountain men were joined by forces under Colonels Cleveland and Winston, bringing the total of troops to about thirteen hundred. After some difficulty in locating the British Commander, Major Ferguson, who had fallen back, it was learned that he had pitched his camp upon a plateau known as King's Mountain which contained about two hundred and fifty acres. Ferguson, after appealing to Lord Cornwallis for re-inforcements, felt secure as he boasted "that only the Almighty could take it from him."[38]

The plan of action followed by the backwoodsmen was to surround the base of the mountain, advance upward under cover of the trees, and

---

[37] Ibid., 146.

[38] Ibid., 154.

finally hem in the enemy on top of the plateau, following always the Indian style of fighting. The results of the battle fought on October 7, 1780, are well known. Ferguson was killed, his second in command, De Peyster, ordered immediate surrender. Some one hundred and fifty Britishers were killed; more than eight hundred surrendered as prisoners. Over-mountain losses were probably less than sixty.

After the American dead had been buried, the Wataugans marched back to their home valleys, having accomplished in short order their objectives, but not until they had hanged some of the British sympathizers. Even there the sense of justice of Sevier and Shelby interceded when nine of the more than thirty convicted had been punished. Upon their return to the Watauga the men were joyously received. Little did these mountain people realize the full importance of the battle in which they had just participated. There is accord between both British and American writers that "the battle on King's Mountain turned the tide of the Revolution in the South, and was a material factor in the surrender of Cornwallis at Yorktown the next year."[39]

Civil Affairs

In the years after King's Mountain, the settlers periodically turned their attention to matters of Indian warfare under

---

[39] Ibid., 161.

Charles Robertson and John Sevier and to matters of local concern. There was a constant urge to move westward toward the Cumberland settlements as many had done in 1779 and 1780 under James Robertson and John Donelson. Others followed Sevier farther down the Nolichucky and even beyond into the rich lands of the French Broad, even though that area was still owned by the Indians. More lands were cleared; more settlers, some of them veterans of the Revolution, appeared to take up land claims. The earliest beginnings in education were made when the Reverend Samuel Doak erected a little log cabin for school purposes in about 1780 and thus began the long and honorable history of the first college west of the Blue Ridge—Washington College, earlier called Martin's Academy.[40]

Inasmuch as many of the Wataugans engaged in the Revolutionary conflict, a look at the military reservation act of North Carolina is helpful to an understanding of our subject. This act provided that each private should be awarded 640 acres for his services; to each non-commissioned officer 1,000 acres; and to the higher ranks greater acreage was allotted. This land was to be located in the military

---

[40]Martin's Academy was chartered by North Carolina in 1783; later it was re-incorporated under the same name in 1785 by the State of Franklin. In 1795 the legislature of the Southwest Territory chartered the institution and changed its name to Washington College. Landon Carter was an early trustee of this institution. *Ibid.*, 164.

reservation in northern middle Tennessee. Many great Tennessee fortunes had their beginnings in these military grants and later speculations in western lands. One of Carter County's great land owners was given a boost in his acreage in 1783 when the legislature awarded to members of the Transylvania Company some two hundred thousand acres in the Powell's Valley and Clinch River region. Robert Lucas, an original member, had transferred part of his interests to John Carter who in 1775 had acquired some interest in the company. After John Carter died about 1780, the Carter share passed to his surviving son, Landon Carter, who probably received in excess of twenty thousand acres by this division.[41]

The year 1783 saw the creation of another neighboring county in honor of General Nathaniel Greene. This new county included its present bounds as well as much of the rest of the present state. Jeremiah Lambert, the first Methodist circuit rider to the Holston and Watauga country, made his appearance in the region and reported sixty members at the end of his first year's work.[42]

The State Of Franklin Movement

In 1784 a dream of the over-mountain men was temporarily given a chance of being fulfilled. Since the earliest days the settlers had depended upon themselves; the American frontier naturally developed

---

[41] Williams, Revolutionary War, 225-227.

[42] Ibid., 235.

this characteristic in its people. There had existed, more or less through the years, a definite lack of harmony and community of interest between the westerners and the tidewater gentry of eastern North Carolina and Virginia. It must have been the fond hope of the leaders in the settlements to some day create a government completely independent of the seaboard states and equal to them in every respect. In short, westerners desired separation.

The first hope of a separate state was found in a Continental Congress resolution of October 10, 1780, which declared that any states to be carved out of western lands would be admitted into the union as equals with the original states. In the North-of-Holston villages there was one man, Colonel Arthur Campbell, who openly advocated a separatist movement by circulating a document early in 1782 asking that a convention be held to consider the situation. Little came of the idea of a convention immediately, but the seed had been spread. Fruit would be reaped later.

Word reached the frontiers that Jefferson's Ordinance of March, 1784, called for the division of ceded territory or lands to be divided into fourteen or sixteen states. It provided that the inhabitants could come together for the purpose of establishing a government "Either on their own petition or on the orders of Congress."[43] About the same time the news arrived that North Carolina had ceded her western lands to the central government under certain conditions. At

---

[43] Hamer, op. cit., I, 116.

the discussion of the matter in the legislature some harsh words were spoken concerning the over-mountain people. The easterners called them "off-scourings of the earth, fugitives from justice," and continued that "we will be rid of them at any rate."[44] Such language induced some of the leaders in the west to proceed without delay and without regard to the conditions attached to the cession. These conditions provided that the region would remain under the control of North Carolina until finally accepted by the Congress which was given one year in which to act.

The settlers met in convention at Jonesboro in August, 1784 and declared themselves independent of North Carolina, following in several instances the wording of the 1776 Declaration of Independence. John Sevier was elected president of the new state named Franklin in honor of the famous patriot and statesman, Benjamin Franklin. Sevier was rather reluctant to enter the new state movement, but, being the natural leader that he was, he was urged by his friends to assume the lead. Undoubtedly the prestige and influence of the office was pleasing to his nature. Plans were made to call a constitutional convention later in the year to draw up a permanent constitution.

Conflict and disappointments were soon the order of the new state. In October, 1784, after a rather heated campaign in the several

---

[44] Samuel C. Williams, *History of the Lost State of Franklin* (Johnson City: The Watauga Press, 1924), 27. This is by far the most complete and definitive work on the subject. Hereafter cited, Williams, *Lost State of Franklin*.

districts, the cession act was repealed by the North Carolina legislature before the Congress had had time to act on the grant. The people of Franklin were faced with the possibility of being declared in open rebellion against North Carolina authority, but they chose to continue behind their leader, save only a handful of them headed chiefly by John Tipton who for the next few years was to represent North Carolina authority in the region.

In a brief survey such as this is, it is not possible to go into details. It was a period of utmost confusion, finally culminating in a period of civil strife and actual bloodshed between the Tipton forces and those of Franklin led by Sevier. Two governments existed; two courts levied taxes, and settlers very often paid neither assessment, pretending not to know to which government the tax should be paid. The area later to become Carter County was known as a part of Washington County under the North Carolina government and was created into Wayne County under the Franklin government in March, 1785, honoring General Anthony Wayne.[45] Wayne County continued to exist and function until the collapse of the Franklin movement in the summer of 1788. Two important members of the Sevier administration were from Wayne County. Landon Carter was speaker of the senate, and Thomas Talbot served as clerk in the senate.[46] Undoubtedly the creation and operation

---

[45] Ibid., 58. The new Wayne County also took in present Johnson County and parts of adjoining North Carolina. Wayne was a Revolutionary general and later became famous as Indian fighter in the Northwest.

[46] Landon Carter was a close friend of Sevier and a "thoroughgoing supporter" of the Franklin movement. He was also secretary of the first constitutional convention at Jonesborough, member of the first council of state, and later secretary of state and entry-taker under Sevier. Ibid., 55, 293. The alignment of the Sevier and Carter influences against the Tiptonites in naming Carter County is later seen.

of this county stimulated desire for a separate county apart from Washington County under the North Carolina system of government. The final collapse of the Franklin movement came in late February, 1788, when actual clash between the opposing forces resounded at the Tipton home, about a mile and half from Johnson City on the Erwin Highway, within perhaps a mile of the present Carter County line. The Tiptonites under North Carolina authority won the day, and the separatist movement was defeated. Later Sevier was arrested on the charge of treason, but the proceedings never amounted to anything. He was temporarily disqualified to hold office, but he still had the good will of the over-mountain men.

Historians have ascribed four reasons as to the rise and decline of the state of Franklin. Briefly one writer has labeled them "the democratic, the ingrate, the speculative, and the separatist explanations."[47] Can the movement best be explained as a spontaneous democratic outburst longing for political freedom? Or was it the grasp for power by a group whose thirst could not be quenched and whose ambitions urged them to rebel against the authority of North Carolina?[48] A third view is that advanced by Abernethy who attributes

---

[47] Walter F. Cannon, "Four Interpretations of the History of the State of Franklin," (to be published in East Tennessee Historical Society's Publications, No. 22, Fall, 1950), page 1 of original manuscript just returned from the printers.

[48] James Gilmore expressed the democratic view and John H. Wheeler, a North Carolina historian, pictured the movement as led by ungreatful and power-thirsty leaders against North Carolina, as cited by Cannon, loc. cit.

the greatest cause to the actions of the North Carolina speculators of whom one was certainly John Sevier. The desire of the speculator group to look after and promote their own interests in the western lands as well as Muscle Shoals is the all-explaining factor in Abernethy's eyes.[49]

The explanation brought forward by other more recent historians is that the Franklin movement was one aimed to bring about a separation. Williams in the preface to his *Lost State of Franklin* said:

> Franklin was without doubt the most pronounced and significant manifestation of the spirit of separation which gave deep concern to the national leaders. No other movement for separate statehood reached even approximately, the stage attained by Franklin--that of a *de facto* government, waging war, negotiating treaties and functioning for a term of years in the three great departments that mark an American State, the legislative, executive, and judicial.[50]

Cannon in his conclusions is also sympathetic to the separatist movement interpretation. He wrote:

> . . . the separatist explanation best fits the facts regarding the founding and history of the state of Franklin. As in most cases, there were few angels and few devils. The west was trying to free itself from control by the east, both in government and in economic matters. It wanted freedom to expand, freedom to regulate its Indian affairs, and freedom to control the land for the profit of its own members.[51]

---

[49] Abernethy, op. cit., 87, 89-90.

[50] Page viii.

[51] Cannon, loc. cit., 31-32, manuscript copy.

The same writer summarized Sevier's motives as "desire for speculation; desire to lead the people who trusted him. . . and . . . personal vanity in maintaining the project which he had led for four years."[52]

Tennessee Becomes a State

Late in 1789 North Carolina ratified the constitution of the United States and officially became a member of the federal union several months after Washington had assumed the presidency. At a legislative session on December 12, 1789, the western territory was ceded to the federal government on certain conditions. Some were that reservations for military lands should still be valid, that North Carolina land grants of earlier date should be valid, and that the territory should eventually be admitted into the Union, but as one or more slave states. The United States officially accepted the grant on April 2, 1790, and organized the new region under the misleading name of the Territory of the United States of America South of the River Ohio, more often referred to as the Southwest Territory since it included only the present Tennessee country. Washington appointed William Blount of North Carolina as the territorial governor. Blount assumed his duties in the new region on October 10, 1790. From what later became Carter County Governor Blount appointed

---

[52]Ibid., 32.

Charles Robertson and Edmond Williams as two of the members of the Washington County court.

On the third Friday and Saturday of December, 1793, the governor ordered an election to be held for representatives to the territorial legislature since the area now included more than five thousand adult free male inhabitants. From Washington County John Tipton and Leroy Taylor were elected and were seated as representatives at the session held in Knoxville on Monday, February 4, 1794.

Later an act of the territorial legislature of July 11, 1795, ordered that an enumeration of the inhabitants of the territory should be made. Washington County reported a total of 10,105 inhabitants.[53] The county voted 873 to 145 in favor of formation of a new state. The total population of the territory was more than 77,000 and in accordance with the Ordinance of 1787, sometimes referred to as the Northwest Ordinance, the region was now entitled to be admitted as a state. Elections were called to be held on December 18 and 19, 1795, to elect five delegates from each county to attend the constitutional convention to meet in Knoxville on January 11, 1796. Here Washington County was represented by Landon Carter, John Tipton, Leroy Taylor, James Stuart, and Samuel Handley. Elections were held early in March to elect members to the senate and house of the state general assembly, even though the state had not yet been officially accepted into the Union.

---

[53]Ramsey, Annals, 648. An analysis of the county census shows the following: 2,013 white males over 16 years; 2,578 white males under 16; 4,311 white females; 225 other persons; 978 slaves.

On March 28, 1796, John Tipton was sworn in as Washington County's senator; John Blair and James Stuart represented the county in the lower house.[54]

On June 1, 1796, President Washington signed the bill admitting Tennessee into the Union as the sixteenth state. Speaking of the young state, one of the most recent historians covering the whole span of her history reminded all that

> She was a frontier State, a part of the West rather than of the South. Her population was small and her influence in national councils was insignificant, but in another generation she was to become one of the most populous and politically most influential of the United States.[55]

---

[54]Ibid., 648-652, 658.

[55]Hamer, op. cit., I, 182.

CHAPTER II

GOVERNMENT AND POLITICS

Even before Tennessee had been officially received into the federal union, the area which later came to be known as Carter County was assured of a separate existence. No longer would it be just the upper part of Washington County, the northern and eastern section of that political subdivision. Probably from the location of Jonesboro as the county seat of Washington County in the year 1778, the Citizens of the upper section led chiefly by the Carters, Tiptons, and the Taylors, had longed for the time when they could break away from the mother county and form a governmental unit in which they would have more influence and one whose political center would be closer to their land holdings.

The general assembly of the newly organized state of Tennessee met in Knoxville and passed a law on April 9, 1796, providing for the Creation of a new county out of the northern and eastern section of Washington County. This new county was to bear the name of Carter in honor of Landon Carter, a prominent leader in his own right since the death of his father, Colonel John Carter.[1] The official reason for the creation

---

[1] Tradition says there was some discussion over the naming of the new county. Apparently the followers of Col. John Tipton wished to call it Tipton County. It must be remembered that Landon Carter had been secretary of state under Governor Sevier in the Franklin state. Sevier was now governor of Tennessee; William MacLin, a brother-in-law of Carter, was secretary of state, Carter was treasurer of the Washington District. Col. John Tipton was only the Washington County senator. Under these circumstances it seems that the Carter influence was the more powerful. However, it cannot be denied that the Tipton influence in the early history of Carter County was great-- a factor with which any historian must reckon.

of the new county is found in this official language, namely: that the citizens of that area "labored under considerable difficulties and inconveniences in attending courts, general musters, elections and other public duties."[2] The boundaries of the new county were to be laid out by Nathaniel Taylor and Joseph Brown and included much more than the present area of the county. Specifically, it included all lands east of the following line:

> . . . from a point on the North Carolina-Tennessee line due north to strike the house of George Haines [sic.], thence by the nearest direction to Buffalo Mountain, thence along the heights of Buffalo, to a high knob near the north end thereof, thence in a direct line to Jonathan Tipton, Jr.'s residence leaving it within the bounds of Washington County, thence in a direct line to the south bank of the Watauga River at Jeremiah Dungan's ford, thence due north to the Sullivan County line.[3]

This included a part of what is now Unicoi County and all of the present counties of Carter and Johnson. It contained approximately seven hundred square miles and extended about thirty-five miles northeast to southwest and was about twenty miles wide.[4]

---

[2] George Roulstone (com.), *Laws of the State of Tennessee* (Knoxville: George Roulstone, 1803), Chapter XXXI, 1796, pp. 100-102.

[3] Ibid. Brown and Taylor were to be allowed $2.50 per day for surveying the line; markers were allowed $1.00 per day. It is interesting to note that these same reasons, official and unofficial, were operative in the establishment of Johnson County about 40 years later.

[4] Eastin Morris (comp.), *The Tennessee Gazetteer* (Nashville: W. Hasell Hunt & Co., 1834), 25. Johnson County was cut away in 1836 with an area of about 340 square miles; Unicoi County took away about 80 square miles in 1875 leaving the mother county with a present area of about 300 square miles.

Location of County Seat

For the purpose of locating a county seat the legislature appointed a commission of five who were to proceed at once "to appoint, fix on, and lay out a place the most suitable and convenient . . . for the purpose of erecting a court house, prison and stocks for the use and benefit of the county."[5] This committee consisted of Landon Carter, Reuben Thornton, Andrew Greer, Sr., Zachariah Campbell, and David McNabb. They were "to contract and agree with suitable workmen for erecting and building . . . a court house, prison and stocks."

This committee chose as the proper site for the new county seat a fifty-acre tract at the foot of Lynn Mountain, east of Doe River, about a mile above where the river empties into the larger Watauga.[6] The name selected for the town was Elizabethtown in honor of Elizabeth MacLin Carter, wife of Landon, for whom the county had been named. This tract of land was divided into seventy-seven lots the majority of which contained one-half acre. At least two lots and the town square which contained about one and one-half acres were

---

[5] Roulstone, op. cit., 101.

[6] Again tradition says that the Taylors wished to locate the county town site on their lands on the Watauga River about two or three miles below the present site of Elizabethton. Apparently the Tiptons sided with the Carters in locating the town site on lands of Samuel Tipton, son of Colonel John Tipton, within easy distance of the old John Carter home. Perhaps the compromise also included that the name for the town should be Elizabethton in honor of Mrs. Carter. Judge Williams, dean of Tennessee historians, said in his little volume, <u>Brigadier-General Nathaniel Taylor</u> (Johnson City: Watauga Press, 1940), that the town was first called "Elizabeth," but he did not cite any authority. (p. 9). The writer has frequently seen the name of the town spelled "Elizabethton."

reserved for use of the county. The others were sold at public lottery under the supervision of Landon Carter, a John Carter, and Nathaniel Folsom.[7] Numbers were placed in a container of some sort. After paying Tipton $10.00, the buyer chose a number which entitled him to the lot in the original plan bearing that number. This fact helps to explain why those who purchased more than one lot found their property located in widely scattered sections of the town plan.[8]

By an act of the legislature passed October 23, 1799, this fifty-acre tract was "to continue to be a town, agreeably to the plan of said commissioners, filed in the Clerk's office of the said county," such town to be known as Elizabethton. Samuel Tipton's deeds of conveyance to the commissioners were made "good and valid" in all courts of law and equity.[9]

To enable the county to pay the expenses involved in furnishing the necessary public buildings the legislature enacted a tax levy.[10]

---

[7] History of Tennessee (Nashville: Goodspeed Publishing Company, 1887), 909. Hereafter cited, Goodspeed, op. cit. This source gives the date of the lottery sale as October 6, 1796, but the writer has found at least 13 deeds to town lots bearing date October 4, 1796. Deed Book A (Register's Office, Elizabethton).

[8] About 20 lots were sold at the lottery sale; during the following year Tipton disposed of 13 more. He continued to sell town lots until about 1820 at prices ranging upward to $15.00 and $20.00 as real estate prices advanced in the town. Some of the earliest purchasers were John Reneau, John Carter, George Emmert, Thomas Lackey, Abel Pearson, Daniel Harkleroad, Joseph Mason, Landon Carter, Abraham Tipton, Jacob Miller, John Brown, James Lacy, and Joshua Roiston.

[9] Edward Scott (comp.), Laws of the State of Tennessee (Knoxville: Heiskell and Brown, 1821), I, Chapter V, 637.

[10] Ibid., Chapter XXXI, 1796, p. 557. Tax rate was as follows: $12\frac{1}{2}$ cents on each 100 acres of land and on each white poll between 21 and 50 years of age; 25 cents on each town lot and on each slave between the years of 10 and 50. Ibid.

This provided for a two-year collection by the sheriff or other collectors and provided for strict accounting as in the case of all public money. Apparently the tax to be levied over the two-year period was insufficient to meet the cost of construction of the court house inasmuch as a tax rate for 1799 included a levy to complete the construction.[11] The building was probably begun immediately and completed without much delay. Like most public buildings on the frontier, it was probably constructed of logs and stood on the town square. It remained sufficient for the needs of the new county for the next twenty-five years until it was replaced by a two-story building.

Early County Court

The first court was composed of the existing magistrates, commonly called esquires or justices of the peace. It included Andrew Greer, Landon Carter, Nathaniel Taylor, David McNabb, Zachariah Campbell, Guttredge Garland, John Vaught, Joseph Lands, and Reuben Thornton.[12]

---

[11] A total of $866.72 was collected for the courthouse as follows: 1796--$271.18; 1797--$143.25; 1796--$160.16; 1799--$292.13. Account Book, 1796-1835 (County Court Clerk's Office, Elizabethton).

[12] Goodspeed, op. cit., 908. Some of these had probably held a squire's commission since the days of the state of Franklin under one authority or another. Unfortunately the minutes of the first years of the county court activities are not available; fires and maybe theft have destroyed many historical records of the county. It might well be that in 1880's when the Goodspeed history was written that these original records were then available.

In accordance with the Tennessee constitution this court proceeded to elect the officers necessary to carry on the business of the county and to keep the peace.[13] This first court, in accordance with the law establishing the county, was held at the house of Samuel Tipton. Later courts were to be held at places which the court would from time to time designate. At a meeting of the second court Nathaniel Folsom were allowed $50.00 as expense money for laying off the town into lots.[14]

The 1796 constitution provided that two squires should be chosen from each captain's company of the militia and from the town district where the county seat was located there was to be an extra justice of the peace and constable. From a study of minutes of the county court

---

[13] The first county officers were:

Sheriff	— Nathaniel Taylor
County Court Clerk	— George Williams
Register of Deeds	— Godfrey Carriger, Jr.
Trustee	— John MacLin (McLin)
Ranger	— Joseph Lands

The earliest constables were:

Charles Colyer	Thomas Whitson
Aaron Cunningham	Solomon Campbell
Samuel Musgrove	John Robertson

Ibid., The writer has seen all these listed in the earliest county records such as minutes, wills, deeds, etc. All were elected for a term of two years except the ranger who served during good behavior. As to their successors through 1861, see table in the appendix, Infra., 182.

[14] Ibid. More early pioneer names of this county are preserved in the panel of the first grand jury: William Dugger, Jules Dugger, Joseph Ford, John Worley, Stephen Redman, John Poland, James Range, Michael Hyder (Jr.), John Peoples, and Robert Lusk.

for the years 1804-1805, the earliest records which have survived, the names of eleven magistrates are given.[15] This suggests that there were five companies of the militia. A list of these early magistrates appointed by the legislature is to be found in the appendix.

The work of the county court was legislative and judicial in nature, consisting chiefly of electing the county officials, appointing committees to lay out new roads, appointing overseers of the roads already in operation, fixing the tax rate and arranging for the collection of all taxes, the emancipating of slaves under certain conditions, and trying cases of a judicial nature. One of the court's duties which touched every property owner was that of levying taxes. We do not know what the tax rate was between 1798 and 1803, but that of the year 1804 may be taken as representative of the earlier years of the county's history:

State Public Tax		County Tax	
On each 100 acres	$0.12½	100 acres	$0.18
On each town lot	0.25	town lot	0.36
on each free poll	0.12½	free poll	0.18
on each slave	0.25	each slave	0.36
On each stud horse sum equal to the season of one mare		each peddler or hawker	5.00

---

[15] This court included, in addition to McNabb, Thornton, Vaught, and Andrew Greer, the following, most of them added in 1801: Archibald Williams, Andrew Taylor, Hugh White, Alexander Greer, Alexander Doran, Thomas Maxwell, and Joseph Thompkins. Minutes of the County Court, 1804-1805; Senate Journal, 1801, p. 167. Scarcely more than four or five ever sat at one time. The number of magistrates was probably increased to thirteen about 1805. At that time we find the county divided into six taxable districts, the militia companies of Captains Grisham, Tipton's old district, Campbell, Anderson, Kay and Thompkins. Minutes, 1805, p. 148, (County Court).

County Poor Tax			Tax for Standards of Weights and Measures		
100 acres	–	$0.06	100 acres	–	$0.04
town lot	–	0.03	town lot	–	0.08
slave	–	0.06	free poll	–	0.04
free poll	–	0.03	slave	–	0.08
			stud horse	–	0.12½ [16]

The Tennessee constitution of 1796 provided that no one hundred acres of land could be taxed at a higher rate than any other, except town lots which could be taxed at a rate equal to two one-hundred acre tracts of land; the poll tax was not to exceed the tax levied on one hundred acres, and the tax on slaves was not to be greater than the tax on two hundred acres.

The manner of assessing and collecting taxes in those early days of the county is both interesting and unusual to a person of the present day. A case on record is that for the year 1805. Here the court ordered certain of the squires to make a list of the taxable property in the various captains' districts, to wit:

David W. Noble, Esq.	in	Capt. Gresham's district
Andrew Taylor, Esq.	in	Capt. Tipton's old district
Alexander Greer, Esq.	in	Capt. Campbell's district
Josiah Campbell, Esq.	in	Capt. Anderson's district
Alexander Doran, Esq.	in	Capt. Kay's district
Reuben Thornton, Esq.	in	Capt. Thompkin's district [17]

---

[16] County Court Minutes, May 15, 1804, pp. 57-58. The following year the county tax was reduced from .18 per one-hundred-acres to .12. The tax for standards of weights and measures was a special one for the year 1804 only.

[17] Ibid., February 12, 1805, p. 148. From the county court clerk's report we are able to see the growth of the militia, reflecting as it did the number of free male inhabitants. He reported in 1813 seven companies, in 1817 eight companies, in 1825 nine companies, and later when the county was divided into civil districts about 1836 there were ten companies. State Archives, Nashville.

When these company lists had been compiled and the property assessed, they were then handed over to the sheriff, and it was his duty to make the necessary collections. Later he would settle with the county trustee.

Later Courthouses

At the May session of the county court in 1820, it was decided to sell the old courthouse building and construct a new one. For this purpose the court appointed a commission made up of Jeremiah Campbell, William B. Carter, James Keys, Alfred M. Carter, and Johnson Hampton. These were "to draft a plan, superintend and contract" for the construction of the new building. They were also empowered to sell the old building at public or private sale at such terms as would be to the best interest of the county.[18] The enabling act of the legislature provided that the different courts were to convene in whatever building in Elizabethton the sheriff might secure. Business to be conducted at this place was to "be as good and effective as if done in present court house, on the public square, and law, usage or custom to the contrary notwithstanding."

---

[18]Scott, op. cit., II, Chapter 36, 1820, p. 645 and County Court Minutes, May, 1820, p. 147. It was about this time that the first of two petitions to the legislature was presented praying that the seat of justice for the county should be located in a site more centrally located for the benefit of those in the later Johnson County area. This will be discussed at length in connection with the establishment of Johnson County, infra., 41-45.

In 1851 or about thirty years after the construction of the second courthouse, growth of the business of the county as well as the deterioration over the years made it necessary to erect a larger building. A committee of seven men were appointed to attend to this matter. It was their duty "to superintend the building of a courthouse . . . with full power and authority to settle upon a plan . . . contract for the building thereof, for a sum not exceeding five thousand dollars in addition to the brick and lumber now in the old court house."[19] The commissioners were not to draw upon the county for more than $800.00 per year until the debt could be paid.

The contract was let to John Lyle and William M. Flemming who agreed to construct the building according to the plans and specifications as drawn up by Joseph S. Burts.[20] Lyle agreed to do the "brick work and plastering and all that pertains thereto" while Flemming agreed to "do all the balance of the work." The contract called for the expenditure of $7,100, $3,700 to be paid to Lyle and the remainder to Flemming. The increase in the cost of construction necessitated a change in the method of financing the project. The court agreed to

---

[19] County Court Minutes, April, 1851, p. 112. The courthouse committee consisted of John Wright, Albert J. Tipton, Godfrey Nave, Christian E. Carriger, Lawson W. Hampton, Richard C. White, and Carrick W. Nelson.

[20] Ibid., January 1852, pp. 144-45. The contract between the commissioners and these two men was signed September 5, 1851, and called for the completion and delivery of the building on or before January 1, 1854.

appropriate $1,000 per year for six years and then $250 during the seventh year.[21]

Upon completion the building was a three-story structure. The brick floor in the "town hall or basement story" was one foot above the level of the pavement on the street. The different county offices and the court room took the first and second floors. The Masonic Order used the lodge room on the third floor.[22] Malcolm N. Folsom was elected caretaker of the building in 1855, and for his services he was allowed forty dollars per year.[23] Afterwards Folsom, Abraham Tipton, and James L. Bradley were appointed a committee to attend to the beautification and convenience of the public lot nearby. These improvements consisted of erecting some horse racks, planting a number of locust trees, and building a "privy house."[24]

---

[21] That makes a total of $6250 of the $7,100. The difference was made up from the sale of lumber and brick out of the old building. Also the court ordered the sale of some property recently purchased from Edmond Williams, the upper half of the jail lot, and ordered three small buildings on the courthouse lot to be rented.

[22] The earliest Masonic Order in Carter County was Kennedy No. 63, authorized December 12, 1826. Later Kennedy Lodge No. 72 was authorized June 7, 1828, but there is no mention of this lodge after that date. In 1838 Kennedy No. 63 is listed as a delinquent lodge. In 1847 C. W. Nelson was a delegate from Kennedy No. 63 to the Annual Communication. The present Masonic Order, Dashiel Lodge No. 238, was authorized October 3, 1854. Charles A. Snodgrass, Freemasonry in Tennessee (Nashville: Ambrose Printing Company, 1944), 285, 488, 491.

[23] County Court Minutes, July, 1855, p. 346.

[24] County Court Minutes, January, 1861, p. 468.

Creation of Johnson County

By 1820, or about a generation after the establishment of Carter County, discontent of the people in the upper parts over the inconveniences of distance and geography began to make itself felt. Taking advantage of the opportunity when the county was about to build a new courthouse in Elizabethton, these citizens of the more remote sections of the county petitioned the legislature for the removal of the county seat to a site more centrally located. Feeling perhaps that this petition might carry some weight in the legislature, the people of Elizabethton and surrounding communities countered with a petition signed by three hundred and five male inhabitants asking that the seat of justice remain in Elizabethton. They pointed out that the present site had served adequately through the years, that town streets and lots had been improved, that an academy had been constructed which served as both school and church, and that a bridge had been constructed across Doe River--all these things at considerable expense to the residents of the county. Such reasoning must have impressed the legislature as the county seat remained at Elizabethton. The new courthouse was constructed, and the agitation over the removal of the county town was silenced for a while.[25]

---

[25] This petition with 305 signatures, clearly legible, is to be found in the Petition and Memorials, Tennessee Archives (War Memorial Building, Nashville), hereafter cited Tenn. Archives. It is undated but referred to an act passed by the last legislature dated May 9, 1820, enabling Carter county to construct a new courthouse. It can, therefore, be assumed to have been submitted to the 1821 legislature. It is unfortunate that the first part of the petition is very fragmentary.

To the legislature of 1829 the people living in the outlying parts of the county again submitted their grievances, and this time they came near achieving their goal--that of removing the seat of justice to a more centrally located site. This time a total of three hundred and ninety-nine citizens signed a petition calling attention of the lawmakers to the "inconveniences under which we labor" as well as the "hardships which we have to encounter" when they had to make a trip to the county seat. They described for the general assembly their situation and the location of the courthouse. In a county of more than six hundred square miles, the courthouse was five or six miles from the county line on the north side, eight or nine miles on the west side, and from forty to fifty miles on the south and east sides. Some residents had been forced to travel forty or fifty miles to attend court; whereas for the people in the lower part of the county, it was only a journey of not more than nine or ten miles.

This time they cited the dangers and inconveniences connected with crossing Doe River "eight times," a stream "very rapid and difficult" and even "dangerous one half of the year." Also they pointed out that it was necessary for some people to "pass five or six miles on foot over steep and difficult mountains." They argued that the site of Elizabethton was such that "no line of communications from one section of the county to another can ever pass through it." They urged that the courthouse and lot be sold and that another location nearer the center of the county be secured.

It appears that a legal technicality saved Elizabethton as the county seat. The Committee of Propositions and Grievances, to which the petition was referred, reported the matter as "unreasonable" and denied the petition because the citizens of the county did not comply with the provisions of a statute requiring "the same to be advertised six months in each captain's company."[26]

Having failed at least twice in trying to locate the county seat more favorably to their interests, the people concerned most in the move then began to plan for the establishment of a separate county. This matter came to the attention of the legislature when Joseph Powell, senator from Carter and Washington, introduced in 1835 a petition of sundry citizens of Carter County "praying a division of the said county."[27] The bill, calling for the creation of a separate and distinct county from the east of Carter to be known as Johnson County in honor of Thomas Johnson, a resident of that section of country for about thirty years, was introduced by Powell in the senate in December. In the lower house of the general assembly, the same bill was introduced by Mr. Samuel W. Williams, member from Carter, whereupon Mr. Bewley moved to strike out the name "Johnson" and substitute therefor the

---

[26] This petition is in the form of a scroll at least three yards in length. It, too, is undated but evidence indicates that it was submitted to the 1829 legislature. It is made up of four parts, two hand written and two printed, the whole pasted together. Tenn. Archives.

[27] *Senate Journal*, October 20, 1835.

word "Taylor."[28] In the same discussion Mr. Campbell of Rhea County moved to strike out the word "Decatur" as the proposed name for the new county seat and insert the word "Johnsonville."[29] A third amendment was submitted by Williams asking that the county seat be selected by "February" instead of "March." Having passed the house on the final and third reading, the bill as amended was returned to the senate for concurrence.

The proposed house amendments brought forth extended remarks from Senator Powell about the name of the new county. He reminded his colleagues that

> we were requested to give the county the name of Johnson in honor of a worth and respectable citizen who spent his life in that party of the county . . . They had all known or been acquainted with the character of Mr. Johnson, who was one of the oldest settlers of the county, and had doubtless sustained through life the character of an honest man. He was a neighbor and a fellow-citizen of most of the memoralists; they had cherished the recollections of his virtues, and were disposed to confer a mark of respect upon his memory.[30]

Powell continued that, so far as he was personally concerned, he would like to have agreed on the amendment changing the name of the county to Taylor. He reminded his fellow-senators that Colonel James P. Taylor, in whose honor the house wished to name the new county, had been one of his good friends, and that his decease had been a great loss to him; but, he added, "my personal inclinations" must "be controlled by the

---

[28] *Nashville Republican*, January 2, 1836.

[29] *Ibid.*, January 5, 1836.

[30] *Senate Journal*, January 5, 1836, 263 ff.

will of my constituents."[31]

A committee of three senators, composed of Robertson, Ledbetter, and Johnson (from Robertson and Montgomery counties), met with a house group in an attempt to harmonize the differences between the two versions of the bill. No record of the compromise proceedings is available, but from the bill which became a law a few days later when signed by Governor Newton Cannon,[32] it is possible to ascertain what must have happened. The name "Johnson County" was restored and the county seat became known as "Taylorsville,"[33] thus the new county honored two early pioneers, Thomas Johnson and Colonel James P. Taylor,[34] leading men of their community.

---

[31] Ibid., Powell, in his remarks entered at length on the Senate Journal and reprinted in the Nashville Republican on January 9, 1836, described Colonel Taylor as "Possessing talents of no ordinary character, his liberal and generous feelings, his exuberant wit, and never-failing humor, enabled him to enchain the affections of all who came within the sphere of his intercourse."

[32] The writer has seen the original bill as filed in the Tennessee Archives and such insertions and changes as described are noticeable. The law further provided that William Gott, sheriff of Carter County, Robert Reeve and James O'Brien were to be appointed commissioners to locate the county seat before March 1, 1836. From 10 to 100 acres were to be purchased as a town site. They were to lay off the town, sell and collect for the lots. The various courts until permanent quarters could be established for them were to meet at the house of the late Thomas Johnson. Local Acts, 21st General Assembly, 1835-36, Chapter XXXI, January, 1836.

[33] About 1885 the name of the county seat was changed from Taylorsville to Mountain City, a name very appropriate considering the location of the town.

[34] The writer wonders how many grade school children of his own area have noticed that a prominent Tennessee history textbook author, Robert H. White, Tennessee Its Growth and Progress (Nashville: Robert H. White, 1936), 690, gives to Cave Johnson the honor in the naming of Johnson County. White probably followed A. P. Foster's earlier Counties of Tennessee (Nashville: Department of Education, 1923) which made the same mistake.

Civil Affairs

For the two decades between 1810 and 1830 few references to the political and governmental activities of Carter County have been found. George Williams, the county court clerk, in his report to the state legislature reported only seven magistrates. He also let it be known that the county had a total of six hundred and seven qualified voters, men over twenty-one years and eligible to vote for members of the general assembly.[35]

Another report of the following year giving the legislature information concerning how much taxes the state treasury could expect during the year from the county is revealing in its political and economic implications, chiefly the latter. A total of $219 in taxes would be paid from the county. An analysis of this report gives us a more complete picture of the county at this time:

```
81,201 acres of land @ 12½¢ per 100 acres      $101.50
   51 town lots in Elizabethton @ 25¢ each       12.75
  412 free polls @ 12½¢ each                     51.50
  155 negro slaves @ 25¢ per slave               38.75
   10 stud horses                                14.50 [36]
```

Another aspect of the political situation in the county is indicated by the congressional election of 1815, that is, the manner in which elections were held. Andrew Taylor as sheriff reported that he

---

[35] The clerk reported the 607 eligible voters distributed in the captain's companies as follows: John S. Williams, 134; John Williams, 104; John Nave, 75; Jeremiah Campbell, 48; Johnson Hampton, 100; Reuben Thornton, 57; and Alexander Doran, 88. At this time Washington County had a total of 1315 eligible voters while Sullivan had 1072. Tenn. Archives.

[36] Tenn. Archives.

47

had held elections on the third and fourth days of August at the courthouse in Elizabethton and at the home of Thomas Johnson on Little Doe a branch of Roan's Creek. In this election a total of five hundred and thirty-four votes were cast. Samuel Powell received Carter County's vote over John Rhea.[37] It appears that only a limited number of polling places, perhaps only the two, were in use until about 1830. The sheriff reported only the two places in the 1827 elections, but in the 1831 elections he reported elections "held at the different precincts." The county court clerk reported a total of nine hundred and four eligible voters for the year 1826. In the 1827 election a total of seven hundred and sixty-six votes were cast, and in the election of 1831 a total of one thousand and twenty-two votes were marked.[38]

Changes After 1834 Constitution

Democratic government in a much larger measure came to the people of Carter and the whole state of Tennessee as a result of the 1834 constitution.[39] This new constitution provided for the popular

---

[37] The vote stood 445 for Powell as compared with 89 for Rhea. In the 1815 elections Christian Carriger was Carter's selection for the state legislature. Same voting places were mentioned. Tenn. Archives.

[38] County Court Clerk's report, 1826; sheriff's reports for the years 1827 and 1831. Tenn. Archives.

[39] It will be remembered that Carter's representative, the Honorable William Blount Carter, was chosen as president of this Constitutional Convention and played no small part in the writing of that instrument.

election of many of the local officials with stated terms of office-holding as contrasted with the earlier method of the election of these officials by the county court. Now the people elected the justices of the peace, the constables, the sheriff, the trustee, the register of deeds, and the circuit and county court clerks. The court continued to elect such minor officials as the coroner and the ranger, but these were no longer to serve for life but only for two years. The register of deeds, the circuit and county court clerks were to be elected for four years; the sheriff and the trustee, for two years; and the magistrates, for six years. Regular county elections were to be held on the first Saturday of March in even years. The election of the governor, congressional representatives, and state legislative officials was to be held on the first Thursday in August in odd years.[40]

In accordance with the 1834 constitution Carter County was divided into civil districts replacing the old captains' companies as the smallest political unit. This law provided that if there were in any county "700 qualified voters and under one thousand," then it would be divided into ten civil districts.[41] To divide the county into districts of convenient size the general assembly by joint

---

[40] William H. Combs and William E. Cole, *Tennessee A Political Study* (Knoxville: University of Tennessee Press, 1940), 22 ff; *Public Acts*, 1835-1836, Chapter II, January 16, 1836.

[41] *Public Acts*, 1835-1836, Chapter I, passed December 3, 1835. The establishment of Johnson County by this same legislature had reduced the number of qualified voters by possibly four hundred.

resolution appointed James Keys, Lawson White, Jeremiah Campbell, Taylor McNabb, and Christian Carriger. These men completed their work and transmitted to Nashville a plot and description of the ten civil districts. With one exception this remained the political division of the county for nearly forty years.[42]

The county election was duly held on the first Saturday of March and later, March 23, 1836, Governor Newton Cannon commissioned the twenty-one justices of the peace for a term of "six years from the first Monday in May 1836."[43] Having seen the original civil district plat and knowing the general area in which these newly elected magistrates lived, the writer presents in the appendix the districts, their general location according to the community or village, and the names of the justices for the period 1836-1842.

Until the election of the county judge at the very end of the period under study, probably the most important man in the county, politically speaking, was the chairman of the county court. Three men who held this position, each for a period of four years, were Isaac P. Tipton, Thomas Gourley, and George Emmert.[44] The legislature

---

[42] On October 1, 1855, Alfred C. Peoples, Amos Davis, and Ezekiel Grindstaff were appointed commissioners to lay off the new eleventh civil district to be made up of parts of the old third and fourt districts. Joel S. O'Brien was also appointed but did not serve. The new district included the "Limestone Cove and Sciotha sections" with elections to be held in Limestone Cove at "the Davis school house." County Court Minutes, October 1, 1855, p. 350, and January 7, 1856, p. 360.

[43] Manuscript on file, County Court Clerk's Office, Elizabethton. For the districts, location, etc., *infra.*, 186.

[44] In the appendix the reader can find a list of the chairmen for the period 1836-1860. *Infra.*, 183.

in 1857 created the office of county judge to be elected by the people of the county. To that office was assigned the duties of the old three-person or quorum court which had met monthly.[45] Carrick W. Nelson, son of David Nelson, prominent merchant and justice of the peace of the town district, was elected as the first county judge.[46]

As a matter of record the names of the members of the county courts for the periods 1842-48, 1848-54, and 1854-1860 are given in the appendix.[47] Since there was a considerable amount of pride and prestige connected with the office of justice, this list gives the names of the most influential men in each of the districts during this time. The old "squire" in many instances was the little "dictator" in his district.

Incorporation of Elizabethton

Another thread in the history of Carter County is the conflict over the incorporation of the town of Elizabethton. In its many aspects there are glimpses of the social, economic and political life of the community. By an act of the legislature in 1799 the town became officially known as Elizabethton and its first commissioners included Landon Carter, Andrew Greer, David McNabb, Zacariah Campbell,

---

[45] Combs and Cole, op. cit., 156-157.

[46] County Court Minutes, June, 1856, p. 389.

[47] Infra., 187.

Reuben Thornton, Rowland Jenkins, William Cunningham, and Samuel Tipton. These men were given power "to establish the necessary regulations for . . . government" of the newly-laid out town.[48]

During the next few years a few changes in the town commissioners were occasioned probably by death, removal or for other causes. Additional commissioners appointed in 1807 were George Duffield, a lawyer, James S. Johnson, and James Johnson.[49] Five more assumed duties as town commissioners in 1811: Abraham Henry, Samuel Watson, Alfred M. Carter, Nathaniel Blackmore, and Henry Drake.[50]

The last group of town commissioners appointed in 1813 by the state legislature included Charles Reno, Robert Blackburn, and William B. Carter. By the same act the commissioners, with five acting as a quorum, were required to appoint suitable persons "to fill all vacancies that may happen by death, removal, resignation, or refusal to act, as the case may be."[51] This authority was later vested in the county court and that body was given the right to appoint trustees for Duffield Academy.[52]

In a petition dated January 1, 1838, apparently in the handwriting of Thomas A. R. Nelson, ninety-five citizens of Elizabethton

---

[48] Scott, op. cit., Chapter V, 1799, p. 637.

[49] Ibid., Chapter LXXI, 1054.

[50] Ibid., II, Chapter LXXXI, 54.

[51] Ibid., Chapter LXII, 1813, p. 132.

[52] Ibid., Chapter CXXXVII, 1817, p. 393.

asked the legislature to repeal the charter incorporating the town.[53] They complained of paying "taxes without corresponding benefits." None or little was spent on the streets, as most of tax money collected was used to "pay Recorder and Constable two very useless functionaires . . . in a village no larger than this." They believed the laws of the state "adequate to the protection of their lives, their liberty, their reputation and their property." Elections must have been something of a farce. In December, 1836, a total of nine votes were cast. In a village hardly "capable of polling between 40 and 50 voters" the December, 1837, election for the seven aldermen brought out a total of fourteen votes electing these men "to rule <u>the mighty destinies of our little village</u>" for the next year. The petitioners reminded the legislature that they "profess to be true Republicans" and that they "detest all sorts of aristocracy." They complained also of the laws passed claiming that some of them were "conceived in the spirit of the Blue Laws of Connecticut." The one particularly mentioned imposed a fine on any man "who might happen to kiss his wife on Sunday."[54]

The charter of incorporation was repealed in 1838, but about ten years later the matter was brought up in the legislature again.

---

[53] State Archives, Nashville. The act of incorporation was dated October 8, 1832 and was later repealed January 25, 1838. <u>Acts of Tennessee</u>, 1837-38, Capter CCXXXIII, p. 340.

[54] The first three signers were Joseph Powell, David Nelson, and T. A. R. Nelson.

Both sides of the issue are given in the two petitions submitted to the 1851 legislature. The city officers and eleven others advised the assembly that the "streets have been cleansed and improved as rapidly as possible," and that "ordinances for the promotion of health and the improvement of morals of the Town" had been passed and that these had had and still were "having their salutary influence"-among the citizens.[55] It charged that the other petition had been signed by people who were not residents of the town and who were minors "who neither have nor feel any interest in the municipal regulations of the town."

The petition against the charter was signed by W. R. Fitzsimmons and forty-four others and protested that efforts to build sidewalks had only prevented the water from running off the streets. The result was the several "dams in the street"—a nuisance to the public. The grand jury of the county had indicted the mayor and the alderman and they were found guilty whereupon, it was charged, that they had raised city taxes to pay the fine.[56] The charter was allowed to remain despite the vigorous protest.

---

[55]Both petitions are in Tenn. Archives. The one "for" the charter was signed by twenty persons, one of whom was John Miner who wrote, "I signed the other petition without reflection." The first eight names are probably those of the mayor and the seven alderman: W. W. Rockhold, probably mayor since first named, John Singletary, James A. Burrow, Thomas P. Ensor, David J. Ensor, John Jobe, Thomas J. Powell, and James M. Cameron.

[56]This petition was dated February 2, 1852. Tenn. Archives.

In another petition sixteen Elizabethton citizens conceded the principle that the majority should rule, but they claimed "the wishes of those who hold the most town property" and were liable to be severely taxes "should be consulted at least."[57] They pointed out that "many clever and worthy men have signed a petition" asking for the incorporation, but they "pay little or nothing but a Poll tax." Solemnly protesting against the proposed incorporation, they announced that the village did not "contain seventy five voters." However, the town was incorporated by an act passed December 31, 1849,[58] probably being largely the work of Senator Abraham Tipton inasmuch as the petition bears the following notation, the report of the Judiciary Committee to whom the petition had been refered: "some conflict of opinion exists . . . leave the matter to the Senator representing that portion of the State."

Early Newspapers

During the latter part of 1835 there came to Elizabethton a young Methodist circuit rider who was destined to make a name for himself not only in the field of religion but also in the field of politics. This young man, scarcely thirty years of age, was

---

[57] Submitted to the 1849 legislature, the petition was dated December 22nd. These names headed the petition: C. ... Nelson, who appears to have written the petition, Jacob K. Snapp, David Nelson, M. ... Nelson, James L. Bradley, A. M. Carter, and others. Tenn. Archives.

[58] Public and Private Acts, 1849-50, p. 66.

William Gannaway Brownlow who perhaps more than any other man influenced the political thought and public opinion in Carter County.[59] In 1839 he began to edit a political newspaper called the Elizabethton Whig, which was in the following year transferred to Jonesboro and published there for the next ten years. About 1849 he moved his newspaper to Knoxville where it became nationally famous as Brownlow's Whig. This man and this paper had their political beginnings in Carter County.

Before the Brownlow paper there was published in Carter County a weekly, but unfortunately we know little concerning its existence. It bore the title the Elizabethton Republican and Manufacturer's Advocate. It apparently was begun during the early months of 1838 under the editorship of William Gott. It was Whig in its political affiliations and had "some three hundred subscribers" when Brownlow took it over.[60] Closely connected with the paper, probably as publisher, was Mason R. Lyon.

On May 4, 1839, Brownlow and Lyon drew up a one-year contract in which Lyon agreed to "print, publish and deliver to subscribers" a paper which Brownlow would edit. "Exclusive control and management

---

[59] For a more extended treatment of Brownlow while at Elizabethton, see E. Merton Coulter, William G. Brownlow Fighting Parson of the Southern Highlands (Chapel Hill: The University of North Carolina Press, 1937), 34-39. Reference must be made to the attempt to shoot Brownlow on the night of March 2, 1840. Only three copies of the earlier paper are known to be in existence. One copy, dated May 12, 1838, is in the Library of Congress; two copies dated November 24 and December 8, 1838, are in the Massachusetts Antiquarian Society Collection, Worcester, Massachusetts.

[60] Jonesborough Whig, July 10, November 10, 1841.

of the editorial department" was the responsibility of Brownlow who agreed to "devote time to editing . . . as he can conveniently withdraw" from his business interest. For his services Brownlow was to receive one third of the net profits.[61]

The first issue of this new adventure was dated Thursday, May 16, 1839, and was entitled the <u>Tennessee Whig</u>. In it the editor informed his reading public that he lived four miles southeast of "this village," that he was engaged in the iron business which "we cannot and will not neglect," and that he would make selections and pen the editorials "by the light of a candle." He later announced there were "struck 700 copies" of this first number and that subscriptions during a later two weeks period had totaled "upwards of one hundred."[62]

Brownlow gave as his reasons for engaging in this new activity "an unwillingness" on his part "to see the only Whig paper in the District go down" and "a love of country." "An innate regard for freedom of thought and action" and a "deep-rooted opposition to, and hatred of, the high-handed measures of a <u>corrupt</u> and <u>corrupting</u> administration" were also large factors in influencing him into the newspaper work.[63] He lost no time in appealing to members of his party to support his paper:

---

[61] Nelson Papers (McClung Collection, Lawson-McGee Library, Knoxville).

[62] Elizabethton Whig, June 13, 1839. The name of the paper was soon changed from the original Tennessee Whig. It prominently displayed the slate of Whig candidates for office: Henry Clay for President, Newton Cannon for Governor, William B. Carter for Congress, and Alfred W. Taylor for state senator.

We appeal to the Whigs generally, and to those in the Congressional district in particular, with a high and holy confidence, to aid in sustaining our paper; and we promise in return, that their most sanguine expectations shall be realized.⁶⁴

The cost of this weekly was $2.50 a year payable in advance. Time payments could be arranged if desired: $3.00 if paid at the end of the first three months; $3.50, at the end of the first six months; and $4.00, at the end of the first year. The rates for advertising were twelve lines or less for $1.00, and each subsequent insertion was priced at fifty cents. The masthead for the first few issues was "Life, Liberty and the Pursuit of Happiness," but to celebrate the Fourth of July he replaced it with "a more appropriate one, to wit: CRY ALOUD, SPARE NOT." This, in reality, became the watchword for Brownlow in the many years ahead. He was most vicious in attacking his enemies and their policies. His success in the newspaper world was to be amazing.⁶⁵

Before the end of his one year agreement with Lyon, a new contract was drawn because Brownlow had decided that it would be

---

⁶⁴Ibid. He informed his readers that the paper would print "general knowledge, historical incidents, miscellaneous matters of either a scientific, literary, or moral character, which may be considered as subserving the cause of humanity," and that he would "not neglect those secular matters of general interest, which may tend to impart useful information."

⁶⁵One writer has this to say: "That a plain Methodist preacher, with but a limited education and with no training whatever in the newspaper business, should start a weekly paper in a small mountain village like Elizabethton, and that that paper, with an obscure beginning and backed by little capital perhaps until the fame of its editor filled the entire land--seems incredible." Again he describes his great secret as "his force and originality" with a "style that gathered in new readers and new subscribers with every issue of the Whig and held them for life." Col. John Mathes in Nashville American, February 18, 1900, as quoted by R. N. Price, Holston Methodism From Its Origin to the Present Time (Nashville: Publishing House of the ME Church S., 1908), III, 321-322.

better business to move his paper to nearby Jonesboro. Brownlow and Valentine Garland, earlier a journeyman in the Whig shop, bought out Lyon's part of the business, paying him $550.00.[66] On May 7, 1840, Brownlow and Garland published his first issue of volume two at Jonesboro. They announced the following as their agents in Carter County: John Singletary, James W. Nelson, and L. M. Swingle. However, the partnership of Brownlow and Garland did not last long. On August 12, 1840, announcement was made through the paper that this partnership was dissolved, and thereafter Brownlow assumed complete control of his paper and achieved notable success.

Valentine Garland came back to Elizabethton where he had earlier during the fall of 1839 published under the name of "Pompey Smash" a humorous sheet carrying the title of "Token."[67] He was the probable editor of a small semi-monthly paper entitled "Jim Crow" whose editor Brownlow described as a "young man fully competent to the task—one who will render the paper acceptable to his readers."[68]

Later Garland announced through the Jonesboro Whig the prospectus of the Tennessee Mirror which he intended to print at Elizabethton. It was to be a "miscellaneous paper, devoted to Culture, Literature, Morality, Amusement, etc." available at $1.50 in advance per year.[69]

---

[66] Nelson Papers.

[67] Elizabethton Whig, September 19, 1839.

[68] Ibid., September 12, 1839.

[69] Ibid., September 2, 1840.

Brownlow commended the young editor in October of that year for his stand "in <u>roasting</u> the Locofocos [Democratic opponents of the Whigs] alive." He urged people to support the paper and urged Pompey to "let the dirty Vagabonds have it."[70] Garland's weekly[71] seems to have been the last attempt to publish a paper in Elizabethton until W. R. Fitzsimmons began to print the <u>Mountaineer</u> some time about 1855.[72]

Carter County, A Whig Stronghold

Very little can be said with any degree of certainty before 1832 concerning politics as related to the state and national picture. Undoubtedly the people of Carter fell in line with the rest of the new state as early as 1796 in supporting Jefferson and Burr, the Republicans (the present Democratic party). Certainly the people of the county must have applauded the election of Andrew Jackson as Tennessee's lone representative in the 1796 congressional election. Undoubtedly the sympathies of the county as well as the state were more in harmony

---

[70] <u>Jonesborough Whig</u>, October 28, 1840.

[71] In December, 1840 Garland removed to Marion, Virginia, where he published a political paper entitled the <u>Harrisonian</u>. Later, about August 1843, he appeared in Athens, Tennessee, with the intention of publishing a Whig paper there to be known as the <u>Hiwassee Republican</u>. <u>Jonesborough Whig</u>, December 9, 1840, August 30, 1843.

[72] Millard Fitzsimmons, Sr., a grandson of the publisher, told the writer that he once was in possession of a copy of the <u>Mountaineer</u> bearing the date "1857." Mr. Fitzsimmons carries on the family tradition and occupation by operating, with the help of Millard, Jr., the Fitzsimmons Printing Company of Elizabethton. Formerly he was for many years connected with the Elizabethton <u>Star</u>, the successor to the old <u>Mountaineer</u>. Interview, July, 1950.

with the Republican philosophy of Jefferson and his new party rather than with the aristocratic Federalists. Westerners and frontiersmen always supported local government as opposed to centralization as advocated by the Hamiltonians. It can also be inferred that Jefferson's good friends and successors, Presidents Madison and Monroe, likewise were the choice of Carter's early pioneers.

In the presidential election returns of 1832 Carter County voted 509 for Jackson, the Democrat, as compared with only 7 for Clay, the National Republican.[73] It will be remembered that Jackson had been the Tennessee legislature's choice as a "favorite son" in the hotly contested election in 1824. Later Jackson ran victoriously against his 1824 opponent, John Quincy Adams, in the presidential election of 1828. Since Jackson was the popular hero of the War of 1812 against England and was, besides, a favorite son, well known and loved by all, it certainly can be said that Carter County went "all-out" in his support in the three elections, 1824, 1828, and 1832.

Between the election of 1832 and the one in 1840 an almost mass transformation of public opinion regarding the Democratic party and Andrew Jackson took place in Carter County as it did in many other counties within the state. A new political party called the Whig had been born principally in opposition to Jackson and his policies. The creation of the Whig party was almost complete in the county and in the state by the 1836 election, but it was not until sometime later that

---

[73]Goodspeed, op. cit., 358.

the Whig forces all over the United States were able to unite into a strong national organization.

Let us compare the election statistics for Carter County for the three elections—1832, 1836, and 1840. We will have to consider Johnson County returns for the last two elections in order to complete the analysis since the Johnson people voted in the Carter elections the first time and in their own the last two times. Such an analysis gives us this picture:

Carter	1832	Jackson-Dem.	509	Clay-Nat. Repl.	7
Carter	1836	Van Buren-Dem.	46	White-Whig	495
Johnson	1836	Van Buren-Dem.	24	White-Whig	169
Carter	1840	Van Buren-Dem.	99	Harrison-Whig	837
Johnson	1840	Van Buren-Dem.	49	Harrison-Whig	390 |[74]

A question of major proportions confronts us in this situation. What caused the unprecedented growth of the new Whig party? Why did the Democratic party literally "go to pieces?" Stating the question a little differently, How does one account for the growth of the opposition party by more than seventy times between 1832 and 1836 or more than one hundred and eighteen times between 1832 and 1840? Then still another question confronts us. This one has baffled an authority on the subject of growth of the Whig party in Tennessee. Abernethy traces the growth of that political party but says that he is "unable

---

[74] Ibid.

to account" for the "decided and persistent Whigism of Carter County" in view of the fact that her "neighbors were strongly Democratic."[75]

A quick review of the situation in Tennessee about 1836 reveals that one after another of the leaders of the state had broken with President Andrew Jackson and his followers. These included David Crockett, idol of the western section, John Bell, prominent among the commercial cirlces of Nashville, Judge Hugh Lawson White, whose political prestige . . . was second in Tennessee to that of Jackson alone,"[76] and Newton Cannon, later to become governor of the state, and Ephraim H. Foster, speaker of the lower house of the legislature for a time. Jackson lost a number of prominent supporters when he opposed and killed the Second Bank of the United States. Still more Tennesseans turned from him when he favored Martin Van Buren as successor. The Democratic stand against federally-aided internal improvements and Jackson's determined stand against the nullifiers in South Carolina were telling blows to that party's support in Tennessee.

Probably the first and foremost reason for the decided switch in political alignment of the voters in Carter was the Democratic opposition to banks and to internal improvements. Two petitions to the state legislature give us a good indication as to the way Carter citizens were thinking. The first urged that body to establish a branch of the state bank at Jonesboro. They pointed out that since

---

[75] Thomas P. Abernethy, "Origin of Whig Party in Tennessee," *Mississippi Valley Historical Review*, XII, No. 4 (March, 1926), 521.

[76] Ibid., 508 et passim.

Carter and Johnson were "largely engaged in Manufacture of iron," their "six blast furnaces and twenty forges" and other machinery were all moving sluggishly "for want of capital and banking facilities."[77]

The second petition plead with the general assembly to expedite and expand the internal improvement program. The petitioners expressed full confidence in the "great advantages of a system of internal improvements." Anticipating the Tennessee Valley Authority's development of this area, they continued:

> While we claim with pride that our country is blessed with a fertile soil, and as great water power as any other on Earth, we mourn that what the Great Creator of the World has in his wisdom deprived us of, and left for engenuity /sic./ to work out, has been so long neglected, an outlet for our products.[78]

They concluded this petition by affirming "railroads to be the most efficient means" of accomplishing the desired results. Playing an important part about 1835 and immediately thereafter was the deep concern of upper East Tennesseans that the proposed Cincinnati and Charleston railroad project might pass through their area. As a matter of fact T. A. R. Nelson, then located in Elizabethton, in a letter to Robert Y. Hayne, President of the railroad company, impressed him with the desirability of locating the railroad through Carter County and the adjoining North Carolina country. He declared that if the county were provided with transportation facilities, that it alone "could manufacture

---

[77] Tenn. Archives, undated, but must be about 1835. Signed by sixty citizens.

[78] Ibid., undated, but submitted to the 1835 legislature.

enough iron to supply the whole United States."[79] This, then, fits into the political picture of the state as Abernethy saw it, for he said a county would go Whig "which stood the best chance of profiting from the establishment of banks and the building of turnpikes and railroads."[80]

A second influence at work in the interest of the Whig party was the matter of personalities. In the election of 1836 it was the sly, aristocratic Martin Van Burean of far away New York versus Judge Hugh Lawson White of Knoxville, running as the independent Whig nominee in this state. White was well known in the county and was related to the Nelsons, a brother-in-law to David Nelson, a magistrate and merchant, a good Presbyterian and Masonic lodge member. Through the influence of David Nelson and his family, including three sons who were very prominent, namely, T. A. R., Carrick W., and Moses W., the cause of the Whig party undoubtedly was furthered. Added to the Nelsons we have the Carters and Taylors who had "all been Whigs in politics."[81] These along with a few others composed the "court-house influences" who were usually "able to determine the stand of the counties, for the simple farmers . . . were uninformed and easily led."[82]

---

[79] Stanley J. Folsbee, *Sectionalism and Internal Improvements in Tennessee 1796-1845* (Knoxville: The East Tennessee Historical Society, 1939), 118 citing letter dated April 18, 1836, from the Nelson Papers. It will be remembered that Hayne had become nationally known as a result of the Webster-Hayne debates in the U.S. Senate.

[80] Abernethy, loc. cit., 518.

[81] Oliver P. Temple, *Notable Men of Tennessee* (New York: The Cosmopolitan Press, 1912), 89.

[82] Abernethy, loc. cit., 510.

Certainly a third factor promoting the growth of the Whig cause in Carter County was the influence and activities of Brownlow's political paper. Prior to establishing his paper he had written anonymously in support of internal improvements and contributed the articles to a Jonesborough paper. His paper was started in Carter County; he continued after moving to Jonesboro to print a considerable amount of news concerning that county, indicating a large subscription from that section. His influence among them certainly must be taken into account.[83] Brownlow championed the principles of Clay and Webster. One writer explains the continued Whig vote of East Tennessee and the influence of Brownlow among them in this manner:

> Virtues of the American System /were/ attractive to a people whose commerce was was bounded on three sides by mountains, and on the South by Muscle Shoals, and when the virtues were expounded to them in the language of the pulpit, they voted the Whig ticket. Against the Democrats and their works the Parson railed in much the same fashion as he did against the devil and his wiles.[84]

---

[83]The writer has heard this story which illustrates the point exactly. Mr. Pierce Julian, now about 84 years old, remembers hearing his father tell stories concerning Brownlow's Whig. James N. Julian, grandfather of Pierce, was a regular subscriber and the children always affectionately referred to the Whig as "Dad's Bible." Personal interview, June 24, 1950.

[84]William B. Hesseltine, "Methodism and Reconstruction in East Tennessee," East Tennessee Historical Society's Publications, No. 3 (1931), 43.

Presidential Election of 1844

Inasmuch as the election of 1844 is one of the most interesting and spectacular of those conducted during this period of our study, let us devote some space to describing its aspects in Carter County. It will be remembered that in this presidential election the Whigs were campaigning to elect the popular Henry Clay of Kentucky while the Democrats were trying to elect a Tennessean, James Knox Polk, a good friend of former President Jackson. The Whigs all over the nation were making an all-out effort to put their man in the executive's seat since their nominees elected in 1840 did not turn out so well. Unfortunately for them President Harrison only survived his inauguration by about a month, and President John Tyler of Virginia turned out to be a Democrat in Whig's clothing although elected on the Whig platform.

Early in January the Carter Whigs assembled at Elizabethton to nominate delegates to attend the Whig State Convention at Knoxville and the National Whig Convention at Baltimore.[85] Two months later T. A. R. Nelson opened the presidential campaign in the county by addressing a meeting held "in the large Presbyterian Church"; and a call went out in April addressed, "WHIGS OF CARTER ATTENTION!!"[86] calling on them to meet for the purpose of organizing a County Clay Club. At

---

[85]Those elected to attend at Knoxville included Robert Love, N. G. Taylor, C. W. Nelson, John Jobe, John H. Hyder, Samuel W. Williams, Christian E. Carriger, Hamilton C. Smith, and Abraham Tipton. Those who were to attend at Baltimore were N. G. Taylor, Robert Love, Samuel P. Carter, David L. Stover, H. C. Smith, William Williams, and William Dean. Jonesborough Whig, January 10, 1844.

[86]Ibid., March 13 and April 17, 1844.

a meeting in May civil district vigilance committees were appointed. These were to organize district Clay Clubs. Responsible for their organization in the various districts were:

First District	-	R. C. White, D. Stout, and Smith Campbell
Second District	-	L. L. Wilson, Elisha Smith, and James W. Lacy
Third District	-	L. W. Hampton, M. Grindstaff, Alex. Lacy
Fourth District	-	W. W. Smith, D. Keener, Thomas McInturff
Fifth District	-	S. W. Williams, S. D. Patton, Jonathan Pugh
Sixth District	-	J. Cooper, Thomas P. Ensor, N. G. Taylor
Seventh District	-	C. Reeve, David Nelson, Joseph O'Brien, Sr.
Eight District	-	George Emmert, James Hickey, J. C. Lacy
Ninth District	-	Godfrey Nave, Caleb Cox, John Carriger
Tenth District	-	Benj. Cole, Jonathan Lipps, D. Bishop [87]

General William B. Carter was elected president of the county club, and he was assisted by seven vice-presidents. The three secretaries were David Buck, James P. T. Carter, and Isaac P. Tipton. The corresponding committee consisted of C. W. Nelson, M. N. Folsom, and Jacob Cameron. The treasurer was David Carter.

When it was learned that John Bell, Whig elector for the state-at-large, was to address the people of the county at Elizabethton in August, a committee of fifteen leading Whigs was appointed to make special preparations to receive him. The committee arranged for a light horse company and as many citizens as could get horses to meet in Elizabethton on Friday, August 24, and proceed from there to the mouth

---

[87] Ibid., May 23, 1844. Only one such district reported news of its meetings if there occurred a formal organization. The Stoney Creek Clay Club included as president Richard Underwood; the three vice-presidents, Jonathan Lipps, Esq., John N. Harden, and Simeon Forbes; the two corresponding secretaries, Lewis D. Lewis, and James Robertson; and secretaries, Jacob Vandeventer and Robert Cass. Ibid., September 18, 1844.

of Buffalo Creek, there to await the arrival of the Bell party. We have the description of the procession:

> The procession was large--very large-- and showed what Carter could do when once aroused. The Big Bell led the way--the band of music followed--then came the footmen-- and behind them 350 mounted men with banners flying. We were astonished--and at the same time pleased--to see so many old men and farmers in the procession.[88]

To stir the citizens to revival-fever pitch the GRAND RALLY of all the Whigs of the First Congressional District was scheduled to get under way on the night of the third of October with a "splendid Torch Light Procession." It was to continue through the fifth. Brownlow was present at this conclave and later described it for his readers:

> . . . if not the largest--the most enthusiastic and promising demonstration that has yet taken place within the whole limits of the eastern division of Tennessee. . . . It seemed that every Whig in this Congressional District was there on duty for three days and nights . . . . We estimate the crowd at SEVEN THOUSAND, but many of our friends say there were from 8 to 10 thousand.[89]

Two last minutes rallies were held at the Presbyterian Church where Oliver P. Temple of Knoxville, Robert Love, and Brownlow addressed the audience and at the Stoney Creek Camp Grounds. At the former place some two hundred mounted "Locofocos" (Democrats) attempted to break up the meeting, but failed. At the camp grounds some converts to the Whig cause were gathered. A Mr. Crumley, two of

---

[88]Ibid., July 10, August 7, 1844.

[89]Ibid., September 4, October 9, 1844.

the Olivers, a Mr. Saul, and a Mr. Frazier who had theretofore voted for the Democrats had "determined to vote for Clay" and didn't "care who" knew it. Also Isaac H. Brown openly declared for Clay and the Whigs.[90]

Elizabethton was the scene of quite a spectacle the night before election. Announcement was made that on Monday night, November 4, "the Whig Ladies of Carter County will have a Torch Light Procession." The gentlemen were to be present and march in the rear of the procession "to defend them if need be." At the close of the parade a supper was to be served at the Alfred M. Carter house by the Whigs of Carter County. Invitations were extended to the ladies from surrounding countiesto attend. Later Brownlow in his account of the activity wrote that three hundred ladies carrying pine torches marched down the streets and were followed by six hundred men. It "presented truly an imposing affair and was conducted in a most orderly manner."[91]

To complete the account of this election the election returns from the upper East Tennessee counties are given. The Whigs had done their best; they had carried Polk's home state over the Democratic party, but they had lost out to Polk in the over-all national picture.

---

[90] Ibid., October 30, 1844.

[91] Ibid., and November 13, 1844. As contrasted with what took place at a neighboring town on the same night, Browlow reported that William Taylor, a saddler about 18 years old, was inhumanely murdered on the streets of Jonesboro while taking part in such a torch light parade. Ibid.

	Clay-Whig	Polk-Democrat
Carter	740	177
Johnson	388	77
Washington	881	1225
Sullivan	350	1253[92]

The Whigs remained intact as a group in the presidential elections through 1861. When the Whigs ceased to exist as a national party, they appeared locally and in the several states as the Know-Nothing or American Party. In the 1860 election the old Whig vote of Carter County as well as that of the whole state was found under the banner of John Bell and the Constitutional-Union party. The continued strength of the Whigs in Carter County is noticeable through 1861.[93] Generally speaking the Whigs or Constitutional-Unionists became followers of Brownlow, Johnson, N. G. Taylor, and T. A. R. Nelson in trying to save the state from secession. Some of the Democrats became open secessionists, but a great many turned over to the Union side. In a very few scattered cases it is probably true that an old line Whig deserted the cause and took up arms in defense of the southern ideas.

---

[92] Ibid.

[93] Goodspeed, op. cit., 358. The Carter Whig vote in the several presidential elections was as follows:

Year	Whig/etc.		Democrat	
1848	Taylor-Whig	745	Cass-Democrat	129
1852	Scott-Whig	585	Pierce-Democrat	130
1856	Fillmore-American	723	Buchanan-Democrat	228
			Douglas-N. Democrat	15
1860	Bell-Const.-Union	859	Breckinridge-S. Democrat	205

CHAPTER III

RELIGIOUS GROWTH OF CARTER COUNTY

Just as religion played an important part in the settlement of this country, then it can just as truly be said that religion played an important part in the history of Carter County. As a matter of fact one of the first disputes in which a historian sometimes may become involved is that of trying to assign a proper evaluation to the Regulator movement of North Carolina, especially as it related to the exodus of people of Baptist faith to the country over the mountains. It cannot be gainsaid that many of the Regulators or those "of regulating principles" came into what is now East Tennessee. Samuel C. Williams, dean of Tennessee historians, has summed up the influence of the Regulators this way:

> Not only on the waters of the Watauga but also in other parts of what is now Upper East Tennessee they composed an influential part of their communities in the Revolutionary War.

and

> The author's research and study lead to the opinion that over-estimate and over-emphasis have been placed on the Regulators' contribution to the early settlements.[1]

Sinking Creek Baptist Church

The growth and development of religious life in Carter County began with the establishment of the first Baptist congregation. It may

---

[1] Samuel C. Williams, *Dawn of Tennessee Valley and Tennessee History* (Johnson City: The Watauga Press, 1937), 347 and 378. Morgan Edwards and David Benedict, early Baptist historians, played up the Regulators and their subsequent influence in early East Tennessee.

also be said that up to 1861 the Baptists probably had a greater influence upon the life of the county than any other religious denomination. It is not known who preached the first Baptist sermon, but with certainty the first organized congregation and their building can be located. It is probable that some of the Baptist preachers known to have been in the Watauga country such as Tidence Lane, Jonathan Mulkey, Philip Mulkey, Jr., and Philip Mulkey, Sr., preached in what is now Carter County. Then again for some years Matthew Talbot lived among the Wataugans owning property about the mouth of Gap Creek. He was a Baptist preacher and tradition has it that he was the probable founder of the Sinking Creek Baptist Church and pastor from about 1775 to 1783.[2]

Sinking Creek Baptist Church is the oldest church congregation in Carter County, and it is also the oldest church in Tennessee still occupying its original location and foundation.[3] There is also more

---

[2] In this connection it is interesting to note that Judge Williams hesitated to call Jonathan Mulkey the "first Baptist preacher in the Tennessee Country." He continued: "The honor of priority must go either to Mulkey or another whose claims so far have been unregarded by historians of the Tennessee Baptists—Matthew Talbot." However, he added that although Talbot was "a leader among the Wataugans," he "exercised the office of minister of the gospel infrequently" since he was so busy with his plantation and public affairs. To the writer this seems a desired generalization to prove the Judge's point that Buffalo Ridge Baptist Church is the oldest church in Tennessee! Samuel C. Williams, "Tennessee's First Pastor," The Baptists of Tennessee (Kingsport: Southern Publishers, Inc., 1930), 15-16.

[3] Williams, Tindell, and others who claim that the Buffalo Ridge Baptist Church in present Washington County is the oldest church in the State make no pretense that the church occupies its original location. During the winter of 1922-23 the church, without membership and having fallen into a state of decay, was moved and reorganized at Gray Station about three miles from the original location. Samuel W. Tindell, "Tennessee's First Church," The Baptists of Tennessee, 52-53.

than one bit of evidence to indicate that Sinking Creek may be the oldest church in the state of Tennessee. Tradition and circumstantial evidence point to the fact that Sinking Creek is probably older than the Buffalo Ridge Baptist Church. It is the hope of this writer that further research on this point will produce evidence which will definitely establish this honor for Carter County, Tennessee.[4]

The earliest record in existence today specifically naming this church is the letter of dismissal granted to Agnes Talbot, dated September 10, 1785. It is signed by Joshua Kelly, pastor, Timothy Trace, elder, Meshek Hail, deacon, and David Job, clerk.[5]

---

[4] A tradition handed down from Uncle "Hampie" Hyder, a veteran pioneer Baptist preacher for more than forty years, tells that during the winter of 1775 two preachers, John and Charles Chastain, held a revival at the home of Charles Robertson. Matthew Talbot, a local preacher of the same faith, was then instrumental in continuing the work. However, because of Indian raids in the summer of 1776, the services were neglected. Sometime about 1777 or 1778 Talbot reorganized the church and served as its pastor until his removal to Georgia about 1783. Jonathan Mulkey and Joshua Kelly also probably preached at Sinking Creek before 1783. Hyder came into the Sinking Creek Church in 1836, just sixty years after the supposed founding. He would have been in a position to hear from the earliest settlers an eye-witness account of what had happened. Talbot and the Chastains are definitely known to have been Baptist preachers. Judge Williams places the date of Sinking Creek Baptist Church "about 1782." He dates the Buffalo Ridge Baptist Church 1778 on the grounds that the Tidence Lanes were then living on Boone's Creek and they started that church. Is it not just as reasonable to assume that Matthew Talbot organized a church or congregation in the Watauga settlements in 1775?

[5] An older letter from "the Watauga newly constituted the Church of Christ," the name regionally applied to the Sinking Creek Church, is dated July 15, 1785. Samuel Tipton's church letter is found among the church records from Shenandoah County, Virginia, dated September 6, 1783, signed by James Ireland, moderator, and Jeremiah McKay, clerk. Earlier records, which there certainly must have been, have been lost through the years. Mr. Fred Hinkle, church historian, King's Spring Road, Johnson City, is to be congratulated for his interest in preserving the many church records. His assistance to the writer is greatly appreciated.

Confusion in the Sinking Creek Story

Four factors have confused our knowledge of the Sinking Creek Baptist Church and its early history. One authority on the early Baptists in East Tennessee in trying to correct a supposed error in the Holston Baptist Association Minutes confused Sinking Creek in Carter County with a Sinking Creek in Sullivan County, locally known as Little Sinking Creek.[6] The Association records indicate that Sinking Creek was admitted to fellowship in 1820, but Tindell asked how this could be "in the face of the record that Sinking Creek Church [was] represented in the association in 1794." In the association meeting of that year a Sinking Creek was represented by William Wall, William Randolph, and Owen Owens.[7] This could not be Carter County Sinking Creek because these are not the names of people known to have ever lived in Carter County, and more conclusively not one of these names can be found on the membership roll of the church for that period.

A second confusing element in the picture is the fact that the Sinking Creek Church was known by that name locally, but the earliest record of the group in the Holston Baptist Association is under the name of "Watauga River Church." Since the settlement in East Tennessee had long been known as Watauga, and since this church was located near the very center of the settlement, this name would be quite natural, and

---

[6] Tindell, loc. cit., 21.

[7] Minutes of the Holston Baptist Association, 1794, p. 30. Hereafter cited, MHBA.

it no doubt distinguished the place from the other Sinking Creek in Sullivan County. The Watauga River Church was not a charter member of the Holston Baptist Association when it was organized at the Cherokee Meeting House in present Washington County on the fourth Saturday in October, 1786.[8] The Watauga group, however, was represented at the several association meetings between 1787 and 1791 after which time it never appears again.[9]

A third confusing element of the story is the fact that Sinking Creek existed as an "arm" of the Buffalo Ridge Church until 1819. Nevertheless, it continued to perform all functions characteristic of a regularly constituted Baptist church. For instance, it continued to appoint delegates to attend the association meetings, but these always

---

[8] At the second meeting of the Association at the Bent Creek Meeting House Preacher Isaac Barton was instructed to write to Joshua Kelly, pastor of the Sinking Creek Baptist Church, "requesting him to appear at the next meeting" to explain his absence from the previous organizational meeting of the association in October, 1786. MHBA, 4.

[9] Joshua Kelly and James Chambers represented the church at Kendrick's Creek in 1787 and reported 20 members. Kelly, M. Hail, and John Brown represented the church in 1789. Chambers and Brown reported 20 members in May, 1791, but in the fall meeting of that same year William Daniel and Joe Cooper reported only 15 members. MHBA, 6 et passim. It is also noteworthy that John Asplund in his travels to compile a register of all the Baptist churches in the United States in 1790 and 1791 visited the Holston Association area during October, 1791. He listed the "Watoga /sic./ River Church" as one of the churches in the "Deceded Territory of North Carolina." Asplund's Register, 1792, p. 40. (The writer saw a copy of this prized book at the Baptist Publishing House in Nashville. It appears not to have been copyrighted.)

sat as members of the Buffalo Ridge Church.[10] As a matter of fact Solomon Hendrix, a leading layman in the Sinking Creek Church, was an elder in the Buffalo Ridge Church. Two reasons are advanced as to just why this seeming loss of independence of the Sinking Creek Church occurred. After the removal of Kelly and Chambers from Watauga the members were left leaderless and gradually turned toward Jonathan Mulkey and Buffalo Ridge for leadership.[11] It will be remembered that in 1791 there were only fifteen members of the church and there existed throughout the region quite a difference of opinion between the "New Light" and "Regular" Baptists.

Accounting for the fourth element of confusion in the Sinking Creek Church, and in fact in the history of the Baptist people in this early period, was the misunderstanding and intolerance of the "New Lights" and the "Regulars." The former had come into East Tennessee chiefly from Sandy Creek Association in North Carolina and

---

[10] Sinking Creek appointed delegates every year except the years 1812 and 1817, but even in these years the congregation was represented by Leonard Bowers and Abraham Odle and Peter Kuhn, respectively. Checking of the church records and the Association minutes reveals that the following were delegates and probably were the leaders of the congregation: Andrew Greer (1796), Solomon Hendrix (attended nine times between the dates 1801 to 1816), Jonathan Buck (attended seven times between 1804 to 1819). Samuel Tipton attended the 1806 and 1807 sessions. Young James Edens, later a prominent Baptist preacher in Carter and Johnson counties, began to appear in the last years just before 1819. MHBA, 50 et passim; Minutes of Sinking Creek Baptist Church, III, 6 et passim. Hereinafter referred to as MSCBC.

[11] Joshua Kelly removed to the Upper French Broad; James Chambers removed to the Yadkin Valley. MHBA, 1794, p. 43.

were headed by Tidence Lane and the Buffalo Ridge Church. On the other hand it seems that the Sinking Creek or Watauga people were of the "Regular" faith. A letter in the old records tends to substantiate this assertion: "Being assembled to worship God and Considering of you to Gather [sic.] with us who intend to Associate in Virginia at the Regular Association. . . . ."[12] The "New Lights" were characterized by their earnest zeal to carry the gospel to others and by the physical manifestations of their emotional experiences. These were the missionary and evalgelical Baptists. On the other hand the "Regulars" were more conservative in their emotional expression and were more concerned with the doctrinal aspects of their belief.[13] This difference of opinions probably accounts for the fact that Sinking Creek did not become a full member of the Holston Association but rather remained under the "watchcare" of Buffalo Ridge Church[14]

---

[12] Letter from "Washington County Watauga Newly Constituted the Church of Christ" to some church not named; the letter is dated July 5, 1785, and is signed by "Wm. Reno Clerk in Behalf of the Church." Fred Hinkle Collection.

[13] For a more complete discussion of the differences between the "New Lights" and "Regulars" see David Benedict, General History of the Baptist Denomination (New York: Lewis Colby and Company, 1848), 790-791.

[14] It is the opinion of the writer and others that this split over doctrines accounts for the fact that there exist two accounts of the Minutes for the period June, 1797, to November, 1800. Throughout the period there are occasional references to efforts to settle differences between the church and the Buffalo Ridge group.

Sinking Creek Church Constituted

As the years passed, the people of Sinking Creek became restless under the influence of the Buffalo Ridge Church. On March 17, 1810, William Hiter came "to look into /their/ situation" and considered their "privileges not as great as a church ought to be invested with."[15] It was then agreed to send Solomon Hendrix, Samuel Tipton, and Robert Sandford as a committee of the membership to go before the Buffalo Ridge Church and bear a "petition for a greater privilege." This petition was received by the parent organization but action was deferred for the time being. The matter must have been amicably worked out between the two groups, for there is no further record of discontent until almost ten years later.

Beginning on April 17, 1819, another attempt on the part of the church to become a constituted church group was made. The membership discussed the matter until May, 1820, when it was finally decided to send a "petition to the Body to Become a Constitution."[16] In June, 1820, after more discussion it was agreed that the "arm of this church" should enter "into Constitution" and "become a Body Distinct from the Buffalo Ridge Church." Sinking Creek was accordingly constituted with Jonathan Mulkey and Uriah Hunt officiating. The congregation also chose Jonathan Mulkey "to take Pastorial /sic./ care of this Church."[17]

---

[15] MSCBC, March 17, 1810, p. 31.

[16] Ibid., 62.

[17] Ibid., 65.

It should here be stated that Mulkey had served the congregation for many years before this. Sinking Creek as a regularly constituted church from Carter County was officially seated in the Holston Baptist Association at the 1820 meeting with James Edens as the church's messenger or delegate.[18]

At the first meeting of the newly constituted church, with Mulkey as moderator, some important decisions were made. Daniel Stover was appointed clerk for the church (a position he had held since an earlier election on February 19, 1803). Stover and Solomon Hendrix were appointed deacons. The missionary spirit of the congregation was evidenced by a motion made by Jonathan Lipps, a resident of the Stoney Creek area, who requested Mulkey and as many of the regular members as could find it convenient "to set as a church to receive members if any should offer [themselves]" at the next regular meeting of the church, such meeting to be held at the home of Thomas Even.[19] Thus the Sinking Creek Church spread its influence and mothered the Stoney Creek group, which became a separate and distinct Baptist church in 1822.

The influence of the Sinking Creek Church began to be felt in other parts of the county. James Lacy's place, in the Doe River Cove section, the present Hampton community, was the next scene of

---

[18] MHBA., 1820, p. 170.

[19] MSCBC, June 18, 1820, p. 66.

missionary efforts, on the second Monday in October, 1822. Still another mission group was begun by Brother James Edens who requested that the church meet at Nicholas Smith's at the Crab Orchard on the Doe River, just below the present Roan Mountain community. At meetings held at this place in February and August 1824, seven persons were received by experience. These were Sarah Whitehead, Susana Perkins, Rebehak Hammit, James Jones, Nancy Miller, Sarah Bedley, and Nancy Brian who were baptised by Reese Bayless.

A Split in the Sinking Creek Church

Before much could be accomplished at these outpost missions, the body of the local congregation was greatly troubled and divided over a matter arising locally. This split reduced the membership and was a contributing factor in the establishment of the first of the Christian Church (Churches of Christ or Desciples) in Carter County, the Buffalo Christian Church.

The facts concerning the division are relatively simple. One week before a certain Fanny Renfro was to have been baptised by the regular officiating Baptist minister, she was baptised by Jeriel Dodge, a man who was "not of our union." Throughout the early months of 1825 the matter was discussed at length and the church became "divided in sentiment" on whether to recognize the validity of her baptism, it having been performed by someone other than a regularly ordained Baptist minister.

Help was summoned from the neighboring churches, Buffalo Ridge, Cherokee, Indian Creek, Cobb's Creek, and Stoney Creek. Carter church representatives included from Cobb's Creek, Isaac Campbell, John Whitehead; from Stoney Creek, Samuel Tipton, Leonard Bowers, John Nave, and Benjamin White. When organized, Reese Bayless acted as moderator and Nathan Shipley as clerk. Dated April 16, 1825, the report is interesting and is quoted herewith in full:

> . . . on Examination of the case of Fanny Renfro we do unanimously agree that the Baptism administered by Jeriel Dodge is not agreeable to gospel order as practiced by the Baptist Churches. We further do also advise the Church at Sinking Creek to hold Fanny Renfro in the same situation that she stood in the church before she was baptised by the sd. Jariel [sic.] Dodge.[20]

A commitee consisting of Caleb Witt, Joseph Crouch, and James Poindexter, selected by the Holston Baptist Association, met at the Sinking Creek Church and issued the following report:

> Enquird [sic.] into the difficulties of Sink Creek Church find them to be a divided People both in principle and practice. Therefore we do autherize [sic.] that part of the Church which hold the principles on which they were constituted and act agreeable to our Asso. to be the Church & hold the keys of the Church and advise them to Exclude all those who have publickly [sic.] declard [sic.] against the government of this Church and in favor of arian Principles and as many others as will not comply with the advise [sic.] of the asso. after due labour to restore them.[21]

Acting on the advice of the committee, those members who retained the original faith and practices met privately at the house of John Dunlap and proceded to transact business in the name of the

---

[20] Ibid., 88.
[21] Ibid., September 26, 1826, p. 93.

church. They declared against Solomon Hendrix "for advocating the baptism of fanny renfro [sic.] and saying that it mattered not who administered the ordinance so the subject had faith in it," and also because he had apparently agreed previously to abide by the findings of the committee, yet he "afterwards remonstrated against the decision of the committee."[22] Unfellowshiped, or in plain terms, "turned out of the church," were Molly Hendrix, Joseph Renfro, David Pugh, Richard Carr, Edward Henry, and Elly McNabb. The meeting also declared against Molly Humphrey "for joining Millers Church."[23]

For some of these and others the estrangement was only temporary and they were soon received back into full fellowship. Yet others were lost to the Baptist Church and here began the discussions and conflicts which one hundred years ago raged between the Christian and Baptist churches in Carter County.

Ministers Sent Out by Sinking Creek Church

The early Sinking Creek Church had still another influence upon the history of the county. From this pioneer church several men went

---

[23] Ibid., James Miller was granted a letter of dismissal from the Sinking Creek Church on April 16, 1825. The Boone's Creek Baptist Church came over to the Christian Church in almost an entire group as a result of his preaching and became known as Boone's Creek Christian Church. Molly Humphrey had probably joined the Boone's Creek Christian Church. For a discussion of the split in the Baptist Church at Boone's Creek, see Harry Wagner, History of the Disciples of Christ in Upper East Tennessee (an unpublished Master's thesis at University of Tennessee, Knoxville, 1943), 50-53.

out to preach the gospel to the people of the countryside, and, undoubtedly because of their lives, the area became a better place in which to live. Their influence was not limited to the county of Carter but certainly extended in a powerful way into the adjoining counties of Johnson and Washington.

Although evidence is lacking to prove this point, it seems reasonable to assume that Leonard Bowers, one of the early pioneer Baptist preachers in the county, was largely influenced and probably ordained to preach there. His name appears repeatedly throughout the early records as a faithful member. Another family by the name of Buck sent two of its members into the ministry from this church. On March 19, 1803, Jonathan Buck was given "leaves /sic./ of this Church to preach the Gospel," and later received a "written license to preach" at the November meeting in 1806. His relative, Elijah Buck, was granted the "Liberty of the Church to exercise his gift in publick /sic./" and in December 1818, he also became a licensed minister.[24]

James Edens, another of the pioneer preachers and one who labored for many years in the more remote mountainous sections establishing local churches, was ordained to preach on February 17, 1827, with Reese Bayless, Richard Murrel, and Joseph Crouch composing the Presbytery. Young Edens had been received into the church in late 1812.

---

[24]MSCBC, concerning Jonathan Buck, p.1; concerning Elijah Buck, p. 60.

Twelve years later John Dugger, a representative of the Cobb's Creek Baptist Church, appeared and asked that Sinking Creek "take in Consideration the gifts and qualifications of Br. Edens to the minestry [sic.]."[25]

Between 1830 and 1845 no fewer than six preachers went forth from the local congregation to spread the cause of the Baptists. Peter Kuhn was ordained on October 19, 1832. On December 19, 1835, Mathias Broyles was granted permission to preach in the churches of the Holston Association. Another was a man who was destined to spend many long and faithful years in the Baptist ministry in Carter and Johnson counties. Affectionately known as "Uncle Hampie," J. Hampton Hyder was received into the Sinking Creek Baptist Church on January 16, 1836. After educational training at Maryville College in Blount County, Tennessee, he was given on December 17, 1842, the "Liberty to Exercise his gifts in public when ever called on and particular in the bound of this church and as often as he possibly can."[26] Others included Mason R. Lyon from the Watauga Church on August 17, 1839; Henry Nave on May 15, 1840; and William Hatcher on July 17, 1847. Not only to the whites but to the colored people as well did Sinking Creek send messengers, for on Saturday, February 18, 1854, the church "granted William Jobe A man of couller [color] a Letter of dismission also the Liberty to Exercise his gift in publick [sic]."[27]

---

[25] Ibid., August 14, 1824, p. 83.
[26] Ibid., 158.
[27] Ibid., 203.

In a study of this early pioneer church it is only fitting and proper that we should recognize the ministers and clerks. After a careful analysis of the church records, a list has been compiled showing names, dates served, etc.[28]

Membership of Sinking Creek Church

After Sinking Creek was constituted as a separate and independent church, it was represented by one or more delegates in the Holston Baptist Association in each of its annual meetings except the one in 1857 where the church was represented by letter. The membership was steady, generally showing an increase until the peak was reached in 1853 when ninety members were reported. Protracted meetings were held once every two or three years which sometimes accounted for temporary spurts in the membership; for instance, in 1845 twenty-four new members were reported "by experience." After 1853 there were at least six Negroes reported in the membership. Just before the Civil War there was a noticeable decline in membership, falling from eighty-four in 1855 to a low of fifty-two in 1858. Frequent switches in ministers could account for some of the decline.[29]

---

[28] Given in appendix, infra., 188.

[29] MHBA., 170 et passim; scattered references in ibid., II (published). Minutes of the Association were printed locally from 1850 onward; complete bibliographical information on each year's minutes is given in bibliography. A study of the delegates sent to the association meetings has led the writer to conclude that these were the leading laymen in the congregation for the period 1820-1861: James Edens (attended 4 meetings), David Pugh (4), Henry Nave (8), James White (6), William Hatcher (5), Alfred Carr (12), and E. H. Range (5). Two preachers, Jonathan Mulkey and Reese Bayless, and three laymen, Solomon Hendrix, Alfred Carr, and Daniel Stover appear to have been the most outstanding in the history of the church to 1861.

During this period of our study elders and other church officers really took their duties seriously. Members would be "disfellowshiped" or dropped from membership rolls almost at the drop of a hat. Undoubtedly the church was a great moral builder and uplifter in the county. Inasmuch as there are no records available for the Baptist churches outside the town district, and inasmuch as the same general reasons were given by that church when it dealt with its delinquent members; therefore, there are enumerated below some of the most common charges brought against members who were "turned out of the church."[30]

1. "getting drunk" (July 16, 1803)
2. "communed with Presbyterian Brethern contrary" (November 17, 1804)
3. "Drunk and offering to fight" (December 15, 1804)
4. "accused church of unjust dealings with him and went out in a very great rage." (September 14, 1805)
5. "leaving her family in disorderly manner" (June 15, 1805)
6. "offering to fight" (July 18, 1807)
7. "Delinquent from Church meeting" (December 19, 1807)
8. "sin of adultery" (May 19, 1810)
9. ". . . fight . . . beating . . . and running a footrace" (January 16, 1813)
10. "intoxication liquor . . . making use of profane language unbecoming a preacher of the gospel" (November 18, 1927).
11. "Joining Methodist" (November 18, 1827)
12. "disobeyed the call of the church" and "some immoral conduct" (December 20, 1828)
13. "joining another church" (October 17, 1834)
14. "horse raising [sic] and disobeying the call of the church." (November 14, 1840)
15. "Marrying 2nd man while 1st living" (May 18, 1838)
16. "for runing [sic] after Bad women" and for being absent from church and for profane language. (November 14, 1840)
17. "Keeping Bad Company about his house and having too much drinking about his house" (March 19, 1853)

---

[30] MSCBC, dates indicated.

The church played another part in the daily lives of the members. In many instances a "matter of Difficulty" between members of the church, instead of coming before a magistrate's court, was settled through the offices of the church. One example was a conflict between Joseph Tipton and Thomas Maxwell which was brought before the church at the February meeting in 1805. The church appointed a committee composed of Leonard Bowers, Solomon Hendrix, and John Polin to "Labour with them and make report at the /next/ meeting." Two months later this committee reported the gentlemen "having settled it."[31]

Just a final word about the membership of the Sinking Creek Church may be in order. Earliest members included the Greers, the Talbots, the Lincolns, the McNabbs, the Bogards, the Dentons, the Fletchers, and the Hyders. Later members included William Davis, Edmond Williams, Isaac Taylor, William Boyd, John Brown, and John Hammer, the Pughs, the Tiptons, the Loves, and others.[32]

Stoney Creek Baptist Church

The first beginnings of the Stoney Creek Baptist Church, now located in the Carter community, can be traced back to a few gatherings

---

[31] Ibid., February 16 and April 20, 1805, pp. 11, 12. This is just one of the many cases that were constantly being brought before the church.

[32] Fred F. Hinkle, "Sketch of Sinking Creek Baptist," Sinking Creek Baptist Church Records (WPA Project 466-44-3-116, September 1938), 4. This short article and the several interviews which I had with Mr. Hinkle have been most helpful.

at the house of Thomas Even held during July and November, 1820. As previously pointed out this church was an off-spring from the Sinking Creek Baptist Church, the "Mother of Carter County Baptist Churches." Near the end of 1820 at the November church meeting it was agreed "to hold church meeting on Stony [sic] Creek Wednesday before the meeting at Sinking Creek."[33] Reese Bayless was the preacher at these early meetings. By April, 1821, the members, several in number, had constructed or acquired a building in which to hold services, as the "Stony [sic] Creek Meeting House" is mentioned in the official minutes.[34]

During the early months of 1822 the subject of constituting the Stoney Creek group into a separate Baptist Church was discussed by the Sinking Creek Church, and it was agreed that the "Stoney Creek members [should become] a constituted body & as many as feel free are at liberty to join them."[35] Later in the year the Stoney Creek Baptist Church petitioned the Holston Baptist Association for membership in the organization, which petition was granted on the second Friday in August, 1822. To the association the Stoney Creek Church reported a membership of thirty-eight.[36]

From a study of the minutes of Sinking Creek Church it is possible to reconstruct a rather complete list of the charter members of this congregation. This list includes all those who were admitted into

---

[34] Ibid., April 24, 1821, p. 71.
[35] Ibid., March 16, 1822, p. 75.
[36] MHBA, 1822, p. 183.

church fellowship as a result of meetings held on Stoney Creek from July, 1820, through March, 1822. Besides the ones listed in the appendix,[37] the name of Jonathan Lipps must be included since he introduced the motion calling for the church to meet at Thomas Even's house.[38]

This congregation also had a record for mission work. In the records of the Holston Association during the 1850's at least four different gifts are noted: $5.00 in 1850, 1854, and 1856, and $4.00 in 1852. Apparently not all the congregations in the association were of the same mind on this mission question. At the Limestone, Tennessee, meeting of the association in 1852, this mission question was addressed to the gathering by the Stoney Creek Church: "What shall be done with a church that opposes our missionary operations or suffers her minister or members to do the same?"[39]

The Association answered the query and passed on this information to the member churches:

1. Resolved, that we consider the Missionary enterprise as being strictly in accordance with the Gospel of Christ.

2. That we regard a Church or Minister that opposes the same as opposing the Spirit of the Gospel.

3. That we advise any of the Churches connected with this Association, that may be opposed to the cause of Missions or its operation--to examine prayerfully the spirit of the Gospel on the Subject.[40]

---

[37]Infra., 188.

[38]MSCBC, July 1, 1820, p. 66 et passim.

[39]Minutes of the Holston Baptist Association (Greeneville: The "Spy" Office, 1852), 4.

[40]All the Baptist churches in the county were the missionary type as contrasted to the Primitive Baptist groups who were not missionary-minded. For a discussion of the Primitive Baptists see Lawrence Edwards, History of the Baptists of Tennessee(Knoxville: unpublished thesis at University of Tennessee, 1941), 48-70.

In 1851, with a membership of ninety-one, the Stoney Creek Church was host to the Holston Baptist Association which met with them for about four days during the second week of August.[41] The congregation reported a steady growth of membership right up to the end of the period, beginning with a total of thirty-eight members in 1822 and reporting an all-time high of one hundred and thirty-three in 1861.[42] Nothing is available to indicate who the pastors and officers were except the statistical charts in the association minutes. The pastors are listed in the appendix; Benjamin Cole and Jonathan Lipps served as clerks at one time or another during the 1850's.[43]

Watauga Baptist Church

The largest Baptist church in the county at the beginning of the Civil War was the Watauga Baptist Church, located in the present Hunter community. Its history dates back to 1831 when the "Watauga Church newly constituted petitioned for and gained admittance into" the Holston Baptist Association.[44] This group began with a membership of only thirty members and in 1858 reached a record of one hundred and

---

[41] MHBA (unpublished), 339.

[42] Outstanding laymen were Benjamin White, Alexander Head, Jonathan Lipps, and Benjamin Cole. Between 1822 and 1840 White attended thirteen association meetings; Lipps has even a better record--attending twenty meetings between 1831 and 1861.

[43] Infra.,188. It is unforunate that the records of this church were destroyed by fire about 1904. The writer has relied heavily on the minutes of the Sinking Creek Church and the Holston Association in this account.

[44] MHBA, August 1831, p. 220.

eighty-eight. That is a considerable record over a period of thirty years and might be due largely to the work of one preacher, Valentine Bowers. His record of attendance at twenty-seven of the thirty association meetings bespeaks the confidence the congregation must have placed in him.

The records of the Association indicate that at least three great revivals were held during the period of this study. In 1843 twenty-seven members were added "by experience"; in 1847 twenty one others were added; but magnificient results followed a protracted meeting in 1853 when seventy-four baptisms were reported. Five years later another revival brought about forty-nine baptisms;[45] one is tempted to wonder if it was not about this time that the Baptists began to make inroads on the Methodists in the county. A membership of twelve Negroes was reported in 1857 and colored members were part of the congregation even to the beginning of the war.

It is regretable that the writer can only name the families who appear to have been members of this congregation. It must have a history that rivals that of Sinking Creek for interest if one could but find the old records which are said to be still in existence, but the writer was not able to locate them.[46]

---

[45] Ibid., 273 et passim.

[46] Members of the church according to the minutes of the Holston Association for the period 1831-1861 included the John and Henry Naves, the Daniel Stovers, the Jonathan Hathaways, Sol Stover, the I. H. Browns, E. D. Hardin, David, Valentine, R. B. and J. L. Bowers, the W. C. Lyons, the J. P. Van Husses, the A. K. Pearces, the Pleasant Williamses, and the families of J. D. and J. T. B. Nave.

Zion Gap Creek Baptist Church

At a meeting of the Holston Baptist Association in Hawkins County, Tennessee, in 1843, the Zion Gap Creek Baptist Church was admitted as a duly constituted church.[47] The earliest leader and pastor was James Edens, formerly of Sinking Creek. In view of the geography of the county, it is only logical to assume that the Gap Creek Baptists branched off from the Sinking Creek Church. The mouth of Gap Creek is probably not more than two miles from the Sinking Creek Church.

In 1855 the Zion Church, barely twelve years after it had been constructed, served as church host to the entire Holston Association. The congregation certainly must have had a building of considerable capacity; its membership of 92 must have been able to take care of perhaps almost an equal number of visitors. The church had only two ministers during the period 1843-1861--James Edens, probably largely responsible as the founder, from 1843 to 1852, and the year 1854; and J. Hampton Hyder, who served during the year 1853, and for the period 1855-1861. In the absence of the regular pastor who probably served only one Sunday each month, it is likely that two licensed members of the congregation, John Hathaway and J. W. Livingston, filled in and did much to build up the church life. This group was a missionary-minded organization. Contributions were received by the Association in the

---

[47]MHBA, August, 1843, p. 270.

the amount of $3.00 in 1855 and 1857; earlier the church had given $2.50 in the year 1854.

The congregation numbered about seventy at the beginning of the Civil War, having grown from an early start with only twenty-five members. There were several members of the Hyder families in this church; several attended as delegates and one in particular, J. E. Hyder, served as church clerk from 1853 to 1861.[48]

Laurel Fork Baptist Church

Another Baptist Church which was planed by James Edens was that of Laurel Fork which mushroomed about 1837 and then seemed to pass out of existence about 1851. The group was admitted into the Holston Baptist Association and given "the right hand of fellowship" in August 1837.[49] It began with a membership of nineteen; apparently a big revival was stated in 1842, probably held by Edens, and it reported a record-breaking membership of forty-nine, thirty-five of them having come in that year by "experience." However, in 1851 a membership of only eighteen was reported, and thereafter it never appears in the association records. Edens served the church one Sunday each month from its beginning to about 1848.

---

[48] From the minutes of the Holston Association for the period 1843 to 1861 it is learned that other members included Samuel Tipton (Jr.), W. Taylor, S. E. Hyder, H. H. Edens, J. O. L. Hyder, Jessee Hyder, J. N. Hyder, and J. B. Campbell.

[49] MHBA, 1837, p. 241.

A few families gave life and strength to the group and kept it alive. Samuel Tipton (Jr.) was one of these, but he must have moved away or transferred his membership, for he was later an active member of the Zion Gap Creek Baptist Church. Granville Kite, John Lacy, Alexander F. Morton, William Lewis, Elisha Campbell, and W. G. Campbell were leading members of the church inasmuch as they were appointed as delegates to the several associational meetings during the period of its short existence.[50]

Elizabethton Baptist Church

The Baptist believers of Elizabethton organized themselves into a local congregation in the summer of 1842 with Elders Reese Bayless, Valentine Bowers, William Cate, and James Edens making up the Presbytery. On June 21 at a meeting held in the Methodist church building, the church, composed of thirty-one members, was organized,[51] drawing its membership from the town people and the congregations at Watauga, Laurel Fork, and Sinking Creek.

Mason R. Lyon, a printer and sometime local Baptist preacher, read the articles of faith which were adopted "without a dissenting

---

[50] Information taken from the several yearly minutes of the Holston Baptist Association, 1837-1851.

[51] Apparently a protracted meeting had been in progress inasmuch as earliest records show that twelve members joined on April 12, 1842. It would seem logical to conclude that by June 21 the congregation was ready to become organized, possibly delayed awaiting the arrival of the Presbytery. A list of the charter members of the Elizabethton Baptist Church appears on page 189 in the appendix. Minutes of the Elizabethton Baptist Church, page not numbered. Hereinafter cited as MEBC. The Jonesborough Whig of July 6, 1842, reported the organization of this church by "Messrs. Cate and Bayless."

voice," and the congregation proceeded to elect Brother Abraham Tipton as church clerk.[52] It was further agreed to "look out for suitable persons " from among themselves to serve as deacons. Services were to be conducted on Saturday before the fourth Sunday in each month. No regular minister was called since the presbytery offered "to attend us alternately for twelve months or until we make choice."

The Elizabethton congregation petitioned the Holston Association for admission on Saturday, June 25th, sending as their delegates Elijah D. Harden, M. R. Lyon, and Abraham Tipton. The church sent along a contribution of $1.50 for association expenses. At the church meeting a month later a letter from the Association was read and approved, thus dating the Elizabethton Baptist Church as a member of the Association from July 3, 1842.[53]

On August 27, 1842, Thomas C. Johnson and William Huffman were elected deacons, and they were instructed to keep a "list of the male members whose duty it is to support the gospel."[54] Huffman remained

---

[52]MEBC, June 21, 1842, page not numbered. Tipton continued in this position until June 12, 1858, when he resigned asking for a letter of dismissal for himself and his wife. He was succeeded on August 7, 1858, by E. H. Range who continued as clerk until the Civil War disrupted the church records.

[53]That year the Holston Baptist Association met at the Watauga Baptist Meeting House in Carter County and received the Elizabethton Church into full fellowship. Also received at the same session were the Baptist churches recently constituted at Jonesboro, Limestone, and Flagpond, MHBA, July 1842, p. 270. The Elizabethton Church remained a part of the Holston Baptist Association until about 1868 when most of the Baptist churches in Carter and Johnson counties withdrew to form the present Watauga Baptist Association. The war years must have weakened the association relationship.

[54]MEBC, September 24, 1842, page not numbered.

only a short while and he was replaced in June, 1843 by Elijah D. Harden.[55] The earliest trustees were Jonathan Hathaway, Abraham Tipton, Dr. Joseph Powell, and William Stover who were "re-appointed trustees by authority of the church under the authority heretofore given them."[56]

The first regularly elected pastor was William Cate, who was "unanimously chosen for the next year" on July 22, 1843. He agreed to accept the call if the church would "abide by 5th Article of the Church Covenant."[57] It is not known exactly how long he served, but he was succeeded on July 24, 1847, by Martin V. Kitzmiller. During this time it also appears that M. R. Lyon preached for the group, probably as a licensed minister belonging to the congregation.[58]

---

[55] Ibid., May 26 and June 25, 1843, pages not numbered. Jonathan Crouch had also been elected but "declined" the office.

[56] Ibid., June 25, 1842, page not numbered.

[57] Ibid., August 26, 1843, page not numbered. Article Five is interesting: "We will watch over each other in the fear of God to reprove and admonish in Christian charity and brotherly love and communicate of our wordly substance according to our several abilities as shall be to the glory of God in the decent support of the church and the minister." This is part of the church covenant adopted upon organization in 1842.

[58] According to the HBA Minutes, Lyon is listed as pastor for the years 1843 and 1845. A listing of the pastors from this source gives the following:

1.	William Cate	1842
2.	Mason R. Lyon	1843
3.	William Cate	1844
4.	Mason R. Lyon	1845
5.	William Cate	1846
6.	Martin V. Kitzmiller	1847-48
7.	William Cate	1849
8.	William C. Newell	1850-58
9.	William C. Bowers (as licensed minister)	1860
10.	E. Spurgin and W. C. Bowers	1861

Further reference to Lyon is to be found in the petition from the Baptist Church at Silver Creek, N. C. "requesting that Bro. M. R. Lyon should be set apart for ordination which was done." MEBC, December 24, 1844.

It seems natural to assume that the Baptists continued to meet in the Methodist church building for the first year or so. On May 26, 1843, Abraham Tipton was appointed to "ascertain whether we can get the use of the Female Academy to hold our meetings in."[59] There probably was a Sunday School quite early, and the church agreed to meet each Sunday afternoon at four o'clock for "prayer meeting."[60]

The congregation in April, 1847, agreed unanimously that "a house of worship /should/ be built in the town." Thomas C. Johnson, George Emmert, and Abraham Emmert were appointed a committee to select a suitable site for the proposed building. At the May meeting, it was reported and favorably received that a location "South of the C. H. in Mr R_____ lot which if it suits the Church can be gotten." George Emmert and Mark Lacy acted as committee to purchase this property. Later, in June, another group made up of George Emmert, John Bayless, Abraham Tipton, Thomas P. Emsor, and J. H. Hyder were delegated the authority to "superintend the building of the meeting house."[61]

The Elizabethton Church drew much of its strength from in and around the Turkeytown section. In May, 1845, the proposal was made that a church be organized in that place. At the next monthly meeting

---

[59] Ibid., May 26, 1843. Goodspeed, op. cit., 911, confirms the Baptist use of the Female Academy Building for services.

[60] Ibid., June 22, 1844.

[61] Ibid., April 24, May 22, June 26, 1847. Earlier Johnson and Emmert had inquired of the Presbyterians "to see if we can get the use of their building." Ibid., December 24, 1844. Tradition confirms the fact that the Baptists did worship for a time in the Presbyterian building.

after some discussion it was finally agreed on motion of Brother
J. M. Crouch that "as many members as can meet in Turkey Town for
worship once a month and that it be called an arm of this church."[62]
This arrangement continued to exist until January 8, 1848 when the
arm of the church was "called in."

There seems to have been close co-operation between the different
Baptist congregations in the county. On May 31, 1847, a committee
was appointed from the Elizabethton church to consult with the churches
located at Sinking Creek and Watauga "to see if they would like to have
Brother Martin Kitzmiller as their pastor," and also to ascertain how
much "they could contribute to his support."[63] Kitzmiller was called
and the church agreed to have services at eleven o'clock on Saturday
and Sunday of the second week in the month. His salary from this
church appears to have been about $40.00 per year. Later the church
was compelled to petition the Executive Board of the Holston Baptist
Association for "assistance to pay our pastor."[64]

The Elizabethton church was not unmindful of the rest of mankind and appeared quite early as a "missionary-spirited group. In 1851 it ordered at the next communion meeting that a public collection be

---

[62] Ibid., June 21, 1845.

[63] Ibid., May 31, 1847.

[64] Ibid., July 11, 1859, p. 356. Pages of the Minutes were not numbered until the early fifties.

taken for foreign missions; at the spring communion a collection for home missions was ordered.⁶⁵ However, it was later agreed that "our weak churches at home should first be aided and that we send the remainder of the missionary [Funds] to the General Assoc."⁶⁶

A fine neighborly feeling existed in the church among its members who probably had not forgotten that they had worshipped formerly in the building of another religious group. The Elizabethton Church passed a resolution allowing "all denominations of Christians" to use its building when it was not in use, provided that "they would be responsible for any damage done."⁶⁷

The Elizabethton Baptist Church was never large in membership, remaining pretty close to forty. In 1843 it began with forty members; in the early fifties it reached almost fifty, but by the beginning of the war it was reduced to forty-three.⁶⁸

---

⁶⁵Ibid., October 9, 1852, p. 349. A study of the mission contributions of this church as listed in the several minutes of the Holston Association (published and unpublished) shows that Elizabethton in 1849 and from 1851 to 1857 gave $3.00 each year to home missions; in 1854 and 1855 we find additional gifts to foreign mission amounting to $4.00 and $3.00, respectively.

⁶⁶Ibid., June 13, 1857, p. 353.

⁶⁷Ibid., October 9, 1852, p. 349.

⁶⁸From a study of the Minutes of the Holston Baptist Association (1843-1861, published and unpublished) 273, et passim. The leaders of the church were Thomas C. Johnson, Abraham Tipton, Thomas P. Ensor, George Emmert, A. C. Bowers. Other members included Mark Lacy, John Bayless, Jr., Abraham Fulkerson, J. F. T. Gifford, and John Renfro.

The Spread of the Methodists

Having traced the growth and development of the Baptists in the county, let us turn our attention to another religious group, the Methodists.[69] The Holston Circuit, which included the Watagua country, was created in 1783 and Jeremiah Lambert traveled the circuit in that year and was succeeded in 1784 by Henry Willis.[70] Since the present Carter County area was one of the thickly settled sections, it seems altogether likely that one or both of these circuit riders preached within the bound of the later county.

The earliest record of the activities of the Methodists of the county is to be found in a few references to personnel and the geography of the area as recorded in Bishop Francis Asbury's Journal which he kept on transmontane wanderings carrying God's message and Methodism to all who would listen. He made seven trips to the over-mountain country between 1788 and 1796, and he touched lands later in the county at least five times and made significant comments in his writings. Here is what he had to say:

Monday 28 /April 1788/

"About nine o'clock we came to Grear's /Andrew Greer's across the Watauga/

---

[69] Unlike other sections of East Tennessee, Carter County was not greatly influenced by the Presbyterians. No schools were established; only one congregation, the Elizabethton church, was established in the county. For this reason the writer has given the account of the spread of the Methodists first.

[70] Williams, Revolutionary War, 235.

Tuesday 5th [April, 1790]

We came to a dismal place called Roan's Creek, which was pretty full. Here we took a good breakfast on our tea, bacon, and bread. . . . . At length we came to Greer's, and halted for the night.

Thursday 28 [March, 1793]

We made the best of our way to Dugger's ford [Julius Dugger's] on Roans-Creek.

Friday 29 [March, 1793]

We passed Doe-River at the fork, and came through the Gap—a most gloomy scene—not unlike the shadowy death in the Alleghany mountain. . . . but to our sorrow we find it low times for religion on Holstein and Watauga Rivers.

[1797]

I am of opinion it is hard, or harder, for the people of the west to gain religion as any other. When I consider where they came from, where they are, and how they are called to go further, their being unsettled, with so many objects to take their attention, with good health and good air to enjoy, and when I reflect that not one in a hundred came here to get religion, but rather to get plenty of good land, I think it will be well if some or many do not eventually lose their souls.[71]

The Methodists in the county spread from the town center. Elizabethton became the circuit headquarters, and from here Methodists radiated into the various communities of the county. Until about 1820 Duffield Academy building served as a "Union Church" where all the people came together to hear any preacher who happened to come into the village. However, the Methodists soon made efforts to establish

---

[71] Samuel C. Williams, ed., Early Travels in the Tennessee Country, 1540-1800 (Johnson City: The Watauga Press, 1928), 291, 293-4, 298, 305.

a meeting place of their own. John Singletary, a local Methodist preacher and a hatter by trade, took the lead in constructing a log cabin on North Main Street in 1820.[72] This structure was on a lot donated by Singletary and as remembered was about twenty-five by fifty feet, including ten windows, and possessed a double belfry. Until after 1850 this remained the Methodist house of worship.[73]

Under the direction of Singletary and Albert Tipton, another local preacher, a more imposing house was begun on First Street just across from Duffield Academy on a lot given by Singletary. Much of the carpenter work was done by Joe Campbell, a slave, and the brick work was done by John May of Jonesboro and John Collins of Stoney Creek.[74]

---

[72] Information obtained from Mr. George W. Ryan, Elizabethton, a grandson of the founder. John Singletary was born in 1803 and married Mary Ann Johnson, a distant relative of President Andrew Johnson. The Methodist Episcopal Church which was erected on "F" Street in Elizabethton in 1913 was known for many years as the Singletary Memorial Methodist Church.

[73] The bell was transferred to the new Methodist Church on First Street, and the old building remained in the Singletary family until about 1885 when it was sold to D. P. Wilcox who converted it into a barn. Interview with Mr. Ryan, March, 1950.

[74] Mr. Ryan remembers the slave carpenter who, later as a free man, completed the carpentry work. John May was the father-in-law of Captain Daniel Ellis of Civil War fame. According to the Ellis family, Mrs. May passed away while her husband was in Elizabethton doing the brick work. This building was used by the Methodists until 1913 when it was sold for $500 to the Free Will Baptists who still occupy it.

The first mention of the Methodists of Elizabethton in the official Holston Conference minutes is in the account of the meeting held at Kingsport in 1833. At that time the Elizabethton circuit was organized and Preacher D. T. Fulton was assigned to care for the 337 white and 22 colored members of that religious group in the upper East Tennessee area. The circuit at this time probably included all of the present counties of Carter, Johnson, and Unicoi. Two years later when William G. Brownlow, the later famous Union leader and governor of Tennessee, was assigned to the Elizabethton Circuit, it reported to the conference 381 whites and 14 Negroes.[75]

It is interesting to note that 1835 was the last year that Brownlow served as a circuit rider. He seems to have been irresistibly drawn to this location by a certain Miss Eliza Ann O'Brien. One writer of note related that here for once Brownlow "made special effort to be sent" to his next assignment, Elizabethton.[76] On September 11, 1836, before the end of his tour of service, he was married to Miss O'Brien at the "Turkeytown Camp Meeting Grounds" by the Reverend L. G. Marshall. Mr. Brownlow seems to have been very successful, for his wife related many years later that

> . . . everybody said he was talented. He was talked about more than any other young preacher in the Conference, and when he preached at Elizabethton, he had more to hear him than any other preacher.[77]

---

[75] Minutes of the Annual Conferences Methodist Episcopal Church (New York: Mason and Lane, c. 1841), II, 233, 365.

[76] Price, op. cit., III, 435 ff. Miss O'Brien was the daughter of James O'Brien who came to Sullivan County about 1814 from Pennsylvania. He prospered as a merchant at Kingsport for about 20 years, and then he moved to Carter County where he engaged in iron manufacture near Valley Forge. Mr. O'Brien died in 1841.

[77] Ibid., 346.

Brownlow in 1836 joined the ranks of the local preachers who probably were very powerful in stabilizing the growth of the Methodists. In his report to the Holston Conference he informed that body that five local preachers were assisting in the circuit. These undoubtedly included John Singletary, Albert Tipton, David Adams, and Hiram Daily, the latter named also serving as town doctor and postmaster as shown by notices in Elizabethton Whig.

After Brownlow became publisher of the Whig at Jonesborough, he remained interested in the Carter County Methodists. Repeatedly in his weekly paper there appeared notices of camp meetings and their results. For instance, early in 1842 he announced a three-day meeting to be held at Gap Creek and later one to be held at Elizabethton. Since there was a church building in Elizabethton, it can be inferred that there probably was a considerable number of Methodists on Gap Creek and perhaps even a regular meeting place. A regular camp meeting was held in Elizabethton during August, 1842, at which time he reported, "eighty-four persons had joined the Methodist Church, and that a great many had professed faith in Christ." It must have been one of the best the country had ever experienced, for he continued, "greater power we never witnessed." In the year 1843 two camp meetings were announced for the fall, one at Turkeytown and the other at Stoney Creek. Thus it may be seen that by 1843 there were definite Methodist bodies existing in Elizabethton, on Gap Creek, on Stoney Creek, and at Turkeytown.[78]

---

[78] Jonesborough Whig, March 23, April 17, 1842, August 23, 1843.

In 1843 the Reverend A. N. Harris was assigned to the Elizabethton Circuit, which then had a total membership of 736 whites and 48 Negroes.[79] Harris's advertising of his circuit appointments in the *Whig* has enabled the writer to get a good picture of the growth of the Methodists up to that time. Assuming that Harris would preach at the larger centers on Sunday, the writer has ventured to name two other communities where the Methodists were relatively strong, namely, Range and Buffalo Creek, where he spoke at the schools. For a three weeks' period he listed fifteen appointments which are also interesting inasmuch as they throw light on the location of certain schools. The appointments were:

A. N. HARRIS APPOINTMENTS (ELIZABETHTON CIRCUIT)

Date	Place	Remarks
Sun. Oct. 29	Range School House	(About 3 miles above Turkeytown)
Tues. Oct. 31	Brush Creek Camp Ground	(Johnson City)
Wed. Nov. 1	Young's School House	(Robert Young's, near Patton's Chapel)
Fri. Nov. 3	O'Brien's School House	(Head of Gap Creek; might have been 1 mile above town toward Valley Forge)
Sun. Nov. 5	Elizabethton	(Center of the Circuit)
Tues. Nov. 7	Gap Creek	(Near the Big Spring)
Wed. Nov. 8	Limestone Cove	(Davis school at the site of Grindstaff Cemetery)
Thur. Nov. 9	Swingle's	(Unicoi)
Fri. Nov. 10	Rock Creek	(Beyond the Fishery)
Sat. Nov. 11	McInturff's School House	(Probably Erwin)
Sun. Nov. 12	Buffalo School House	(Near Milligan College)
Tues. Nov. 14	Turkeytown	(Near Camp Grounds)
Wed. Nov. 15	Stoney Creek	(Watauga Valley – Hunter)
Fri. Nov. 17	Weaver's	(Just inside Sullivan County)
Sat. Nov. 18	Day's [79]	(Unidentifiable)

---

[79] *Jonesborough Whig*, October 24, 1843.

From the preceding schedule it can be seen that a few appointments on the circuit were in neighboring Sullivan and Washington counties. Another schedule listed, in addition to those mentioned, "Carr's" in Sullivan County and the "Taylor School House" which was located at Okolona on the present Johnson City-Erwin Highway just inside the Carter County lines.[80] Apparently these were two stops on the southern part of the circuit because in the following year the Johnson Mission was established as a part of the Elizabethton Circuit with W. R. Long in charge of the work in that section. In the 1847 yearly reports to the Conference Elizabethton was listed with 524 members on the circuit while the Johnson Mission showed a membership of 213.[81] The influence of the Methodists in the county began to be felt in other sections as their membership increased. In 1850 the Watauga Mission was established in the present Hunter community; this later became the Watauga Circuit in 1853 with William W. Smith in charge of the work. At this time the Elizabethton Circuit reported 504 whites and 35 Negroes; the Taylorsville Circuit, 234 whites and 7 Negroes; and the Watauga Mission, 177 whites.[82]

---

[80] Ibid., June 19, 1844.

[81] D. R. M'Anally, Life and Times of Rev. Samuel Patton, D. D. and Annals of the Holston Conference (St. Louis: Methodist Depository, 1859), 305 et passim. The Johnson Mission became known as the Taylorsville Circuit in 1850. John Early, ed., Minutes of the Annual Conferences of the Methodist Episcopal Church, South (Nashville: Publishing House of the M. E. Church, S., c. 1855), I, 112 et passim.

[82] Ibid., 433 ff.

The 1850 census listed the occupations of the people, and it showed five local preachers and the Elizabethton Circuit rider. These included:

1. William W. Smith, farmer and preacher, age 36, lived in the fourth civil district.
2. John Singletary, preacher, age 41, lived in the seventh civil district.
3. Simeon Forbes, age 36, preacher, lived in tenth civil district.
4. Peter Emmert, age 50, farmer and preacher, lived in eighth civil district.
5. Nathaniel G. Taylor, age 30, preacher and farmer, property value $12,000.00, lived in the sixth civil district.
6. William T. Dorrell, age 29, lived in the seventh district, head of the Elizabethton Circuit.[83]

The career of Nathaniel G. Taylor, the father of the later famous Bob and Alf Taylor, is interesting for its influence on both politics and religion. He was early in life a member of the Elizabethton Presbyterian Church. He wished to become a lawyer as had been his father, James P. Taylor, before him. However, his whole life was changed by the tragic death of his young sister, Mary. She and a male friend were accidentally killed by a bolt of lightning at the Brush Creek Camp Grounds at a Methodist camp meeting. "Feeling that his sister's death was a Divine rebuke for not carrying out the wishes of his mother," who desired that he enter the ministerial rather than legal profession, young Taylor changed his mind and a few days later "delivered a passionate religious address."[84] Brownlow in 1845

---

[83] Seventh Census (1850), Schedule of Population, Tennessee (microfilm).

[84] Paul D. Augsburg, Bob and Alf Taylor Their Lives and Lectures (Morristown: Morristown Book Co., 1925), 18-19; Jonesborough Whig, August 10, 1842. Taking advantage of the strange happening, one preacher took as his text "Meditate on these things," and another chose "But the thunder of his power who can understand?" During the meeting 64 persons were added to the church, Brownlow reported in the next issue, August 17, 1842.

described Taylor as one who surpassed the expectation of his friends, and was "destined to make a successful preacher." He continued the characterization, saying that "he addresses his appeals to the strongest feelings of the heart and is admired for his animating fervor."[85]

The Methodists in Elizabethton were the leaders of the temperance movement, and they organized the Elizabethton Temperance Society sometime before December, 1840.[86] The officers included two Methodist ministers, Hiram Daily as president and John Singletary as vice-president; the secretary of the organization was Jacob Cameron, a Presbyterian.[87] All meetings were opened and closed with prayer. Article Four of the constitution was the important pledge to which each member was suppose to adhere, namely,

> The signature of each member name to this Constitution shall be considered a Solemn pledge that he will abstain from the use of & traffic in all intoxicating drinks unless in cases of extreme necessity to use it as medice [sic] or wine sacramentally & use their influence to get others to do the same.[88]

---

[85] Ibid., August 27, 1845.

[86] The Dailys moved to Marion, Virginia in December, 1840. A sketch of Hiram Daily's life is given in his own publication, Villany Exposed (Marion, Virginia: The Harrisonian Office, 1841), 14.

[87] McCown Collection (Mrs. L. W. McCown, Johnson City)

[88] Ibid. Jacob Cameron, David Nelson, W. Reeve, John Singletary, William D. Jones, J. O'Brien, and Hiram Daily composed the committee which drew up the constitution of the organization.

To the constitution fourteen members immediately appended their names and others probably signed later.[89]

The earliest families connected with Methodism in Carter County, and particularly in Elizabethton, were the Folsoms, Jobes, Crumleys, Singletarys, O'Briens, Burrows, the N. G. Taylors, the Daniel Ellises, the James J. Angels, the Henderson Roberts, some of the Tiptons, Edenses, Toncrays, Collinses, Wilcoxes, and Andersons.[90]

As a matter of record there is inserted in the appendix a list of all those who served as circuit riders on the Elizabethton and Watauga circuits until 1861.[91]

Elizabethton's First Presbyterian Church

Shortly after the coming of the first Presbyterian ministers to the Watauga country, one of them, the Reverend Samuel Doak, made a visit to the Carter section. The occasion proved to be a very

---

[89] In addition to six who drew up the constitution seven others signed the pledge: Thomas Badgett, William C. Daily, James Scott, Phebe Nelson, Mary Nelson, Margaret Cameron, Nancy A. Daily, Elizabeth Daily, Catherine Daily. For some reason W. Reeve's signature is not among the charter members although he helped to draw up the constitution. __Ibid.__

[90] As remembered by Mr. G. W. Ryan and Mrs. M. F. Wilcox, of Elizabethton. It is quite possible that some of those mentioned did not belong to the church before the Civil War period. The names, no doubt, are right, but they may be confused with members of a later date. At any rate the memories of some of the Methodists, advanced in years, are our only source as to who were members inasmuch as not even a scrap of records survives and laymen were not admitted into the conference until about 1885.

[91] __Infra.__, 190.

historic one. To courageous pioneers standing in the fields at Sycamore Shoals, about nine hundred strong in addition to friends and relatives who had gathered to bid them farewell, the Presbyterian minister delivered a powerful and inspirational message. He led the devotions fervently invoking God's blessing to rest upon the expedition as it started to King's Mountain, closing his address with the words of the Old Testament: "The sword of the Lord and of Gideon."[92]

Before there was a regularly organized Presbyterian congregation in Elizabethton, it is evident that ministers from the Washington and Greeneville colleges, in Washington and Greene counties respectively, and probably a few itinerant Presbyterian preachers spoke to groups of people in private homes or in the academy building. One example of this was the message delivered by Dr. Charles Coffin, a business agent of the Greeneville College, when he had been "warmly invited to preach a lecture" before leaving the county in February, 1803. From a text taken from Micah 6:6 he preached "in the evening at the appointed time" to "a number of persons collected" at the home of Mrs. Landon Carter where he had been invited to stay during his visit by young A. M. Carter.[93]

The Presbyterian Church in Elizabethton was "organized by the Rev. L. G. Bell by order of the Abingdon Presbytery in the year 1825."[94]

---

[92]Williams, Revolutionary War, 145.

[93]Tennessee Journals of Dr. Charles Coffin, 1800-1822 (typewritten copy in the McClung Collection, Lawson-McGhee Library, Knoxville), 81.

[94]Minutes of Session, First Presbyterian Church, Elizabethton, Vol. I, 1, undated. Hereafter cited, MFPC.

Upon organization Alfred M. Carter, William D. Jones, and Benjamin Brewer were "elected and ordained Ruling Elders." Indicative of the strength of the Presbyterians and their previous work in the county is the fact that seventeen charter members were received into full fellowship immedidately, probably having come from one of the Presbyterian Churches in Washington County. The Carters and Taylors were the earliest leaders in the organization of this congregation. To the seventeen charter members were soon added twenty-nine others.[95]

The earliest records have been lost, but a brief history of the ministry of the church was ordered to be made a part of the record on June 10, 1859.[96] Besides the regular minister others who preached from time to time, probably supplied by the Holston Presbytery, were J. D. Wilson, R. P. Wells, Henry Smith, S. Sawyer, J. R. King, and Ashbell Otis.[97] One early minister, James McLin, was later president of Washington College.[98]

An early item in the records indicates the missionary-mindness of this congregation. On January 18, 1835, a collection was taken for foreign missions and thirty-three dollars "were collected and paid into the hands of Rev. Jared Avery, Agent for Foreign Missions."[99] Later during the same year more than sixty dollars were raised for Bible Missions.

---

[95]MFPC, I, 1, undated. The names of the charter members and the later twenty-nine are given in the appendix, infra., 191.

[96]For a list of ministers, infra., 191.

[97]MFPC, 41, et passim.

[98]McLin graduated from Washington College in 1818; he received a Master of Arts degree in 1822 and continued with the college as tutor until April, 1828, when he was elected by the Trustees to serve as president in which capacity he served until April, 1838. Howard E. Carr, Washington College (Knoxville: S. B. Newman and Company, 1935), 26-27, 179.

[99]MPFC, 2, 3 (October 6, 1835).

The Elizabethton Presbyterian Church served as host to the Holston Presbytery during April, 1835. As a result of this fellowship the church made substantial growth, increasing the membership by fourteen. In 1837 William R. Rhea, William Gott, and James C. Simpson were elected as ruling elders. Three other important men in the community were ordained as elders in March, 1841. They were David Nelson, Jacob Cameron, and David W. Carter. These and other officials of the church, as was the practice of the day in all churches, took their duties very seriously. When any member walked in a disorderly manner or violated moral or religious precepts, he or she was immediately brought before the "session" or officers and very often "excommunicated" or "expelled" from the membership of the church and from church privileges. Before these officers, members were brought charged with "intemperance and profane language," "conduct unbecoming the christian character," and for other charges more or less serious.[100]

The congregation early went on record against the evils of drink, adopting ringing resolutions, to wit:

> 1. Resolved, that the members of the Presbyterian Church, in Elizabethton, Tenn., will neither use ourselves, manufacture or vend to others any description of ardent spirits except for medicinal purposes.

---

[100] MFPC, 2, 4, 15, 16. Rhea transferred from the Blountville Presbyterian Church. Simpson had been elected in 1833 but declined to serve. Gott served on faithfully until June, 1840, when he and his wife were granted letters of recommendation to the church near Salem, North Carolina.

2. Resolved, that we earnestly recommend to the members of this church, individually and collectively, the adoption of a similar resolution of abstinence from all participation in an evil which involves more <u>crime</u> and <u>wretchedness</u> than perhaps any <u>other</u> practice of the present day.[101]

This resolution was signed by John F. Cunningham, minister, and A. M. Carter, William R. Rhea, Benjamin Brewer, and William Gott. In connection with this resolution, it can also be stated that the Presbyterians were active, along with the Methodists, in directing and becoming members of the Elizabethton Temperance Society.[102]

While John W. Cunningham was minister of the church, the congregation showed real signs of growth and life. A new church building was constructed--a brick building, rather large for the time. According to recollections as compiled by one writer, the building was "completed 1837 at a cost of $1500.00," and the official dedication took place in September of that year.[103]

By 1841 the congregation included "in communion" a total of fifty-two members according to the report the church made to the Holston Presbytery.[104] While growth was being reported, the group

---

[101]Ibid., May 9, 1840, pp. 14-15.

[102]Supra. 108.

[103]Goodspeed, op. cit., 910. It seems strange that the official church records make no mention of this activity at all. It is also interesting to note that political gatherings were at times held in the Presbyterian building.

[104]MFPC, March 19, 1841, p. 17.

also felt the surge of some of its members to go westward. In March, 1843, the session granted letters of dismissal to the Misses Ann E. Huffman and Elizabeth Huffman who were starting for Missouri. Landon D. and Mrs. Emily P. Carter were dismissed to remove to Middle Tennessee.

There has existed a tradition that the religious people of Elizabethton were very cordial one with the other. A letter from James McLin, the minister of the church, to David Nelson, gives us a fine example of the goodwill between groups. In addition it gives us a few facts concerning the church at the time of the writing, February 18, 1844:

> Mr. Nelson,
> Please say to your Sabbath school that there will be no preaching in the Presbyterian Church to-day. Say to the ringer of the bell not to ring.
>
> I did not know this day two weeks since when I appointed to preach today that the Methodist brethern would have a two days meeting at this time. I think that courtesy requires that we omit our meeting.
> I will preach in the Church this day two weeks since and probably for the last time.[105]

Apparently their regular preaching services were omitted for the day, but the Sabbath School, commonly called Sunday School now, was continued. This was a fine gesture of co-operation between two of our early churches.

A scrap of paper survives which gives us a look at the financial condition of the church. For the year 1839, J. W. Cunningham had been

---

[105] Nelson Papers.

paid in cash $139, and there was yet due him for his year's labor the sum of $60.50. This would indicate that he served for $200 per year --two Sundays each month. It is also pretty certain that money was subscribed to pay his salary.[106]

New life appeared in the congregation just before the Civil War. A number of projects were undertaken and partially completed in view of the fact of the troublous times seen in the offing. The session of the church unanimously agreed on May 30, 1859, to call the Reverend J. M. Hoffmeister of Liberty Hill, Hawkins County, Tennessee, "to take charge of this church every two weeks."[107] The members further agreed and pledged themselves to pay him $250 per year for his labors among them. He accepted the call of the church immediately. At the August meeting, 1859, plans were made to ascertain what money, if any, was still in the hands of the women's organization. The

---

[106]Those who paid and the amounts are indicated:

Benj. Brewer	$10.00	Jacob Cameron	$10.00
Eliz. Carter, Sr.	5.00	C. W. Nelson	10.00
W. R. Rhea	10.00	M. C. Taylor	10.00
A. M. Carter	80.00	Mary Taylor	4.00

Those who had not yet paid their subscriptions included:

Wm. Lucas	$10.00	W. Crawford	$ 5.00
Wm. Gott	10.00	M. C. Taylor	10.00
A. W. Taylor	7.50	(had paid $10.00 of her $20.00)	
Wm. Rich	5.00	Mary Taylor	3.50
		(had paid $4.00 of her $7.50)	

McCown Collection

[107]MFPC, 40.

church arranged to procure fifty hymn books and hired the services of a sexton at $1.00 per month.[108]

Then, early in 1860, plans were made and the purchase of a parsonage was completed. The house and lot, "known as the Jack Smith property. . . . formerly Dr. Magee's," was acquired for the sum of $600 "for use of present supply as long as he may continue to minister to the church and then after to be for the use and benefit of this church or whoever may be the minister."[109] By private subscriptions the minister, Hoffmeister, and elder, S. M. Stover, had raised by April 28, 1860, a total of $274.15 and executed a note for the remainder. Dr. James M. Cameron, a deacon, was added to the committee charged with raising the balance as soon as possible. Then the minister, at his own expense, built a study on the parsonage. It was agreed by the session that the minister should be reimbursed to the extent of $150 or he would be allowed to sell it upon his leaving.

During the next year the church was able to pay $119.50 on the parsonage note, leaving an unpaid balance of $207. The report to the

---

[108] Ibid., 42 et passim. Later it was learned that Mrs. Eva Carter was holding some $26.00, "proceeds of a fair for church purposes." This money was applied "towards putting a plank fence around the church, making steps, etc." Seventy hymn books were finally purchased at a cost of $32.00, twenty of which were paid for by the church and the remainder by private subscription. Also two new stoves, purchased from Noff and Coffman, Jonesboro, replaced the old heating system at a cost of $46.00.

[109] Ibid., 45 et passim.

Holston Presbytery in April, 1861, however, showed a membership of only thirty-one. The minister agreed to remain on another year, through April 1, 1862, at his regular salary of $250.

The items of expense for the church for the year ending April 6, 1861, are interesting and reflect a well balanced program: repairs, parsonage, and salary of the minister.[110] It can be imagined that the interior of the church was more beautiful and more comfortable:

7 lamps	$16.00	Turp. brushes etc.	$20.00
Oil	5.00	Repair old lamps	5.00
10 gal. oil	11.75	2 stoves	46.00
Church repairs	22.25	S. Sch. purposes	20.00
Painting costs	39.00	Support gospel	200.00
W. B. Carter		Towards parsonage	119.50
for paints	26.00	Sexton's expenses	7.50
Total			$538.00

The Earliest Christian Churches

Without question the earliest group known as the Disciples of Christ (generally called, however, the Christian Church in Carter County) was the one located on the banks of the Buffalo Creek near the present site of the Hopwood Memorial Church on the Milligan College campus on the old Elizabethton-Johnson City highway. The approximate date for the founding of this congregation can be placed about 1828 or

---

[110]Ibid., April 6, 1861, p. 53.

perhaps even a little earlier. Some of the early members of this group were those who had previously belonged to the Boone's Creek Christian Church, Washington County, Tennessee, which came over in almost a body from the Baptist Church as a result of the preaching and teaching of James Miller who held a revival there about 1828. Other early members were those who broke away from the Sinking Creek Baptist Church because some members of that church would not accept the baptism of Fanny Renfro at the hands of Jeriel Dodge, a preacher unacceptable to the Baptist brethern.[111]

John Wright became the minister of this congregation and through his periodic reports to the Millennial Harbinger, a reformation church paper edited and published by Alexander Campbell, it is possible to follow the growth of the church. In a letter from Elizabethtown [sic] dated March 30, 1833, he wrote, "Our congregation at Buffaloe [sic] Creek, Carter County, in nine months from about forty to near one hundred members.[112] Wright liked to refer to himself as a "reformer," identifying himself with Campbell, Stone, and Scott who were spearheading the "reformation progress." In the same letter he added that

---

[111] One writer concluded that "it seems probable that the organization of the Buffalo Creek Church was perfected as early as 1828" as a result of the differences in the Sinking Creek Baptist Church over the administration of baptism. Wagner, op. cit., 62.

[112] The Millennial Harbinger, IV, No. 4 (April 1833), 237.

"great efforts have been made to counterbalance our labours, for that seems to be the lot of all in the reformation."[113]

Correspondence carried on in the year 1834 between the churches at Buffalo Creek and Boone's Creek indicates that Ira Howard was the clerk of the Buffalo Creek Church. Some loose system of organization and fellowship was in operation at that time, for Buffalo Creek reported that "We have attended our Regular Annual Meeting."[114] During the fall of the same year Michael E. Hyder was elected treasurer of the church. Two old receipts bearing the name of James Gourley record the fact of Hyder's being treasurer.[115]

Three sheets of an old Hyder treasury report are still readable today, and from these a list of some of the early members of the congregation can be ascertained. For the period 1835-37 he listed the names of those who made contributions and the amount of each.[116]

---

[113] Ibid.

[114] It is a lamentable fact for the historian at least that the Christian Churches were such poor record keepers. Since they did "not acknowledge any tribunal above the church /local/," it is impossible to go to conference or association records and find information as is true of other religious groups. Letters, June 21 and September 27, 1834, Kefauver Collection, Boone's Creek, Tennessee.

[115] Dated September 2, 1836, for $13.00 and October 29, 1836, for $3,32½, found in the Professor Sam Hyder Collection (Milligan College, Tennessee).

[116] The treasurer was Michael E. Hyder, grandson of Michael Hider (Hyder), a signer of the Watauga Petition to North Carolina for Protection, 1776, and the progenitor of the many Hyders and related families in Carter County today. Original report is found in the Professor Sam Hyder Collection. For a list of the early members of the Buffalo Creek Church, infra., 192.

Reporting the upper counties in East Tennessee, John Wright mentioned a revival held at Buffalo Creek in late August, 1841, in which he was assisted by James Miller of Washington County. They "gained for the King fifty-three, a part of these from the world, the rest from the Methodists, Baptists, Lutherans, and one from the Universalists."[117] At that time the church had a reported membership of 150. Referring to methods used by himself, James Miller, James I. Tipton, and David Wright, who were the principal preachers in this area among "Christian-Baptists," he wrote that they sought "to enlighten the understanding," and addressed the "sense, and not the passion." He seemed pretty well satisfied with their efforts for they had "succeeded in a getting a full share of the intelligent part of the community" in the reported additions for the three counties, totaling nearly 100.[118]

A statistical account of the information concerning the Christian churches throughout the whole country was issued by Alexander Hall in 1848. It listed the strength of the Buffalo Creek congregation as "186, with house, preacher Elder J. Wright, layman James Gourley."[119]

---

[117]Letter from John Wright, Jonesborough, September 8, 1841, to Alexander Campbell, found in The Millennial Harbinger, V, No. 12 (December, 1841), 590.

[118]Ibid.

[119]Alexander Hall, comp., The Christian Register (Lloydsville, Ohio: Alexander W. Hall, 1848), a copy of which is in the Carolina Discipliana Library, C. C. Ware, Curator, Box 1164, Wilson, North Carolina. This publication listed four other Christian Churches in the county, namely, Turkeytown, Mt. Pleasant (parent organization of the Hampton Christian Church), Crab Orchard (below Roan Mountain), and Stoney Creek (probably the earliest beginnings of the present Blue Springs Christian Church). Concerning the last two congregations no further references have been found which suggest they antedate the Civil War period.

Our next information comes from the 1850 census reports which listed five preachers who were representatives of the Christian churches:

1. Thomas Wright, age 29, born in Illinois, lived in the fourth civil district.
2. John Wright, age 60, farmer and preacher, lived in the fourth civil district.
3. James I. Tipton, age 56, farmer and preacher, property value $4,000.00, lived in seventh civil district.
4. Radford Ellis, age 46, lived in eighth civil district.
5. Peter Emmert, age 50, farmer and preacher, lived in the eighth civil district.[120]

The second Christian Church in the Carter County area was the one established in the Turkeytown section about 1839 or 1840. The distance from this place to Buffalo Creek in Carter County and Boone's Creek in Washington County, then the only churches of this faith in the vicinity, probably dictated the location of this congregation. This early beginning was the parent ancestor of the present Brick Church Christian Church on the Watauga road between Elizabethton and Johnson City.

John Wright in his report to Alexander Campbell, written from Jonesborough, East Tennessee, dated September 8, 1841, mentioned that in August of that year a "four day meeting" had been held with the Turkeytown group which resulted in five confessions. He also stated that fifteen others had been "added this season," making a total of "about ninety members."[121]

---

[120] Seventh Census (1850), Schedule of Population, Tennessee (microfilm).

[121] The Millennial Harbinger, V (December, 1841), 590.

In Alexander Hall's survey of the Christian churches on the country in 1848 the Turkeytown group is listed with 118 members, with a pastor, Radford Ellis, and with the leading layman, probably elder, John Curtis.[122]

Some of the early members included Radford Ellis and family, George Mottern and wife, parents of "Uncle" George Mottern of the Range community today. Others were Jim Range and sons, Jake, Elkanah, Alfred, Henry and Harrison; David Holly and wife, parents of "Aunt" Julie Mottern; Henry Little and wife, Tilda Mottern; Solomon Vest and wife, Susanna Mottern; Riley Campbell, John Hendrix, Louise Arrants, and Jack Lacy.[123]

The 1848 survey of Christian churches listed another in Carter County by the name of "Mt. Pleasant." This is the old name of the present Hampton Christian Church and was located several miles farther up the road leading to Tiger Valley. This early report indicates a membership of fifty members with J. Snyder as the leading layman.

The early records of this congregation have been destroyed, but one writer interested in the growth of the Christian churches in

---

[122] Hall, op. cit.: this publication also listed S(olomon) Synder as the leading layman of the Crab Orchard Christian Church. It is probable that the Crab Orchard group was earlier associated with the Mt. Pleasant Church above present Hampton, Tennessee.

[123] As remembered by "Uncle" George and "Aunt" Julie Mottern, age 88 and 84 respectively, life-long residents of the Upper Turkeytown area. The present Brick Church dates back to about 1866 or 1867; it was completed by the Christians and Baptists after an earlier "Thompson Church" burned a short while after the war. The old "Thompson Church" was the probable meeting place of the Christian Church.

East Tennessee a few years ago found an old entry in the church record that is no longer available. From this entry, which apparently had been recopied from a still older volume, it is possible to learn something about the early beginning of this congregation. The entry was as follows:

> The Church was first organized at the home of W. M. SNYDER. The first preaching was at the home of John Hill. Bro. D. T. Wright and J. I. Tipton in the year of 1842. Second Lord's Day in April. When Wm. Snyder, John Hill and his father confessed Christ followed by others. We then erected a house of worship. Called it Mount Pleasant it was attended for about Seven years by T. J. Wright as pastor /sic/. Also with the aid of other ministers as helpers as follows. S. H. Millard, A. Campbell, John Wright, Jas. I. Tipton and R. Ellis. From Mount Pleasant we moved to Fishers old Field where the Church grew rapidly for a season.[124]

Some of the early members included individual members from the Michael Grindstaff family, some of the Campbells, Hills, Snyders, Halls, probably some of the Lacys, Simerlys, and others.[125]

---

[124] Wagner, op. cit., 79. Oldest residents of the area can remember the old names of Mt. Pleasant and Fisher's Old Field as mentioned by old residents of fifty years ago.

[125] As remembered by "Uncle" Lide Hall, "Uncle" John Campbell and others. Personal interviews, May, 1950.

CHAPTER FOUR

EDUCATIONAL DEVELOPMENT IN CARTER COUNTY

Little concern for education was manifested during the early years of the Watauga settlements. Survival and the fight for liberty became the main concern of the inhabitants. What educational opportunities existed must have been limited to home instruction and training. Most of the early men could read and write as is evidenced by the fact that only two could not sign their names to the earlier mentioned 1776 petition to North Carolina.

The wealthiest inhabitants availed themselves of educational opportunities back in the coastal states. Young Landon Carter was educated at Liberty Hall, Mecklenburg County, North Carolina. Perhaps others attended schools in Virginia and North Carolina, and it can safely be assumed that some children of the early settlers received some formal schooling at Martin's Academy at Jonesboro which had been chartered by the North Carolina legislature in 1783. Landon Carter was one of its trustees and remained an active supporter of the school.[1] Some students from the county also attended Greeneville College.[2]

---

[1] In the first meeting of the Board of Trustees of Washington College after its chartering by the legislature of the Territory South of the River Ohio, Carter was instructed "to dispose of three tracts of land on Doe River belonging to Martin Academy--420 acres donated by Col. Waightsell Avery of Mecklenburg County, North Carolina." Carr, op. cit., 4, 11.

[2] Dr. Charles Coffin, business agent for the Greeneville College, on a visit to Carter County during February, 1803, recorded in his journal, "Mr. Blevins, father of the lad sometime ago a pupil at college, called . . . . to express his desire to send his son back" and "Mrs. Carter, Mr. Blevins & old Mr. Guin would send each a daughter." Tennessee Journals (typewritten copy in the McClung Collection, Lawson McGhee Library, Knoxville).

Duffield Academy

In 1806 a compromise between the states of North Carolina and Tennessee and the federal government resulted in the beginning of a state educational system to be supported by income from public lands. Later during the year the legislature established an academy in each of the counties then in existence.

Duffield Academy, the oldest educational institution in the county, was established in accordance with the state Academy Act of September 13, 1806. This act also appointed trustees for the school. The young lawyer, George Duffield, in whose honor the school was named, headed the board of trustees which included other well known pioneers such as Nathaniel Taylor, George Williams, Alexander Doran, and John Greer, all men of character and prominence.[3] These men were "empowered to fix upon and purchase a site, and to take and receive subscriptions for the same."[4] The act also decreed that the number of trustees should never exceed thirteen, and that the first named, probably acting as chairman, was to fix the time for the first meeting of the group, giving members ten days' written notice thereof.[5]

---

[3] Edward Scott, comp., Laws of the State of Tennessee, I, (1806, Chapter VIII), 931. For a biographical sketch of George Duffield, infra., 193-194.

[4] Scott, op. cit., 931.

[5] Ibid., Goodspeed, op. cit., 911. The next year Andrew Taylor, Abraham Henry, and Reuben Thornton were also appointed trustees. Scott, op. cit., I (1807, Chapter LVI), 1041.

A tradition of the Duffield family places the construction of the first building "about 1809".[6] The 1819 legislature appointed five additional trustees probably replacing some of the original ones who have died or moved from the county. These new trustees were also men who were prominent in civic affairs: James P. Taylor, Alfred M. Carter, William B. Carter, James I. Tipton, and William Graham.[7]

The first concrete account of the activities of the school is found in a petition submitted by Elizabethton citizens to the legislature asking that body not to move the county seat. Three hundred and five petitioners from the town and surrounding sections reported that they had "built by private donation an academy constructed of brick and answering also the purpose of a church which cost them three thousand dollars, and a bridge across Doe River at the west end of the town which cost them three hundred dollars."[8]

---

[6]Interview with H. C. Duffield, Elizabethton, July, 1950. The present Duffields in Carter and Johnson counties are direct descendants of the founder. It is also interesting to note that the street passing the present Duffield Academy school bears the name Academy Street. Though a few yards from the original foundations, the present building, owned by the city of Elizabethton, is located on the original site. A few years ago some of the original foundation stones were gathered and erected into a monument commemorating the early school site.

[7]The Carter influence in operating the academy was great. Two of Landon Carter's sons, Alfred M. and William B., and two of his sons-in-law, George Duffield and James P. Taylor, were members of the board of trustees.

[8]Undated, but after May, 1820, inasmuch as that date is mentioned in body of petition. Tenn. Archives. Goodspeed, op. cit. 911, places the date of the building "about 1820."

A further report of the school is found in the account of the trustees submitted to the county court by David M. Carter and Jacob Cameron, a special committee of the board of trustees appointed in 1848. The committee informed the court that since "the records of the Academy previous to the coming into office of the present board have been so loosely kept (no record Book having been used, and some of the proceedings of the board may have been lost as they were kept on detached pieces of paper)," it would be impossible "to make a full and complete statement of the receipts and disbursements . . . . from its organization up to the present time."[9] They did report, however, that "there came into the hands of William Gott who was a Trustee the sum of $1216.61 on the first of October, 1832." Later there was loaned out on interest $300. This totals $1516.61 "which said sum they put down from the last information they [could] collect as the original amount drawn from the state treasury for Duffield Academy."[10]

---

[9] Original manuscript report of six pages filed in the office of the Register of Deeds, Elizabethton. Hereafter cited, Academy Papers. This report is dated September 2, 1848, and gives an account of the financial conditions of the Academy from 1832 to 1848. The Academy Papers also include several reports and other miscellaneous related material.

[10] The Senate Journal, December 13, 1831, as cited by Harold E. Ward, Academy Education in Tennessee Prior to 1861 (unpublished Master's Thesis at George Peabody College for Teachers, Nashville, 1926), 26, provided that each county in East Tennessee should receive $1,139.76 plus 6% interest for the year 1831. Later $18,000 was to be divided annually among the county academies. Acts, First Session, 22nd General Assembly, 1837-38, Capter CVII, 156. Between the years 1840 and 1861 Duffield Academy received each year about $240.00, its share of the state funds. Ward, op. cit., 34, 35, and Academy Papers.

The committee believed that the academy funds were used "in building the House and in payment of teachers." They referred to the carpenter's work having been done by George Smith, but did not know how much was paid out for that purpose. The report, however, does give some information concerning total costs of building and seats. James I. Tipton had contracted to build the house and seats for $1345.00, there being a balance of $14.20 due him when the seats were delivered on May 28, 1841.[11]

Three teachers are definitely identified by this early report. To the Rev. James McLin the trustee paid $240.00; to the Rev. Stephen Fisk, $106.12½; and to Wood Furman, $22.38, the balance due him.

There was due the school, so the report continued, "in notes all of which are supposed to be good, and cash in hand the sum of $1814.45." The academy then and for years ahead until the beginning of the Civil War carried a credit account, some of which it was never able to collect, as the report of 1850 indicated "due Academy for tuition, at least, the sum of $200.00 most of which cannot be collected."[12]

---

[11] Ibid., Concerning the construction of the building, one account related: "In 1838 the old building was torn down, and a contract for the erection of a new one upon the same foundation was let to P. Q. Satterfield and Solomon Q. Sherfy. It was not, however, until 1841 that the building, which is still standing, was completed." Goodspeed, op. cit., 911. It is probable that James I. Tipton had the contract and sub-let it to Satterfield and Sherfy who hired a carpenter named Smith.

[12] Academy Papers.

Listed as an item of expense was $5.00 paid to W. G. Brownlow for printing, probably for advertising in the Elizabethton Whig. In several issues in the early part of 1840, the terms of tuition were announced: Spelling, writing, arithmetic at the rate of $5.00 per session of five months with Mr. Wood Furman of South Carolina as instructor. A more varied and advanced curriculum was offered to the older students: English grammar, geography, and history, at $7.50 per session, while the Latin and Greek languages, or the sciences were priced at $10.00.[13]

Examination of the pupils in attendance took place on Thursday and Friday, August 20 and 21, 1840, under the direction of Mr. Wood Furman. The results were "creditable to both Teacher and students" and "gave satisfaction to both parents and guardians."[14] Furman's services were engaged for the coming year and announcement was made that the next session would begin on the seventh of the coming September.[15] Perhaps it was because of pay conditions, but for some reason the Furmans did not remain in the county.[16]

---

[13] Elizabethton Whig, April 9, 1840.

[14] Jonesborough Whig, September 2, 1840. A fair estimate of the number of pupils for the year would be 28 or 30, since the 1840 census indicated that 48 students were in attendance at both academies (male and female, this latter to be discussed infra., 132-135.

[15] Ibid., Two of the trustees, A. W. Taylor and W. B. Carter, made the announcement. It is interesting to note that the 1840 census showed only 6 professional people in the county. Of this number Mr. and Mrs. Furman were two of them. Sixth Census (1840), Population Schedules, Tenn. Vol. I (microfilm). As later pointed out, Mrs. Furman was teacher of the Elizabethton Female Seminary.

[16] Twelve others besides Mr. Furman are listed in his household in the 1840 census. Of these seven were under twenty years of age, probably his children or students.

An interesting letter is found in the last issue of the Whig published in Elizabethton. "A Friend of Learning" asked M. R. Lyon, Brownlow's partner, to publish a list of books "wanted for the male and female academies." The writer explained that the list was not "intended to be a complete catalog, but comprised such as are immediately wanted."[17]

The next teacher for the academy was James McLin, a Presbyterian minister and the former president of Washington College. November 15, 1841, was to mark the beginning of the session in a "handsome commodious brick building," just completed in a town known for its "healthfulness" and natural scenery "probably nowhere surpassed."[18] The new teacher was well qualified with his "experience of more than eighteen years in the instruction of youth." Tuition rates were about the same as earlier; sciences were offered at $8.00 per session. Board was to be had with private families in the village for $1.50 per week.[19]

No further notice of the activities of the academy is seen until May, 1845, when the Reverend Stephen Fisk, "well recommended and well qualified to teach the various branches,"[20] became the next teacher.

---

[17] The letter was probably written by one of the Furmans. The list included 28 different books by 21 authors. Latin and Greek books, readers, histories, Walker's Dictionary, Webster's Spelling Book, logic rhetoric, geometry, geology, and the Young Lady's Class Book were requested. Elizabethton Whig, May 14, 1840.

[18] Jonesborough Whig, November 10, 1840.

[19] Ibid.

[20] Ibid., May 14, 1845.

Ministers, according to the general custom, taught the early schools. A woman, Mrs. Hover, was added to the teaching staff of the academy in 1853, but was later replaced by Elizabeth C. Singletary, a local woman. A glance at the list of teachers in the appendix[21] reveals the fact that Hover and his wife together received only about $125.00 per session. An academy teacher earned probably less than $15.00 per month.

More information concerning the session of 1858 is available in the Academy Papers. Twenty students enrolled on February 8 and sixteen others enrolled between that date and April 13. Again "in the last half of the session" twenty-two students began their work on April 19 and were joined by eight others before May 11.[22]

Just what was the purpose of the academy and why did it exist? One writer, after making a study of the rise and fall of the academies in Tennessee, gave reasons which appear likely to have been operative also in the case of Duffield. A summary of the reasons follows:

1. To prepare pupils to enter college;
2. To develop pupils mentally, physically, and spiritually;
3. To develop "highly polished and cultural men and women;
4. To develop mental discipline;
5. To "produce citizenship competent to protect intelligently the best interest of the state and nation."[23]

---

[21] The officers and teachers, as many as are known, are listed in the appendix, <u>infra.</u>, 195.

[22] A list of the students and the amount of tuition paid by each is given in the appendix, <u>infra.</u>, 195-196.

[23] John E. Middlebrooks, A History of the Rise and Fall of the Academies in Tennessee (unpublished Master's thesis at George Peabody College for Teachers, Nashville, 1923), 15.

Not only was the influence of the academy felt in the town, but it also served as a center from which to assist educational efforts in other sections of the county. This is clearly evidenced by the following incident. In March, 1857, Henderson Roberts and James Jett Angel, commissioners of the 26th "Scholastic district," agreed to pay the trustees of the academy $60.00 "for furnishing a teacher to teach the male children within the lawful age for the space of five months." Children were to be subject to the "rules and regulations of the said Academy."[24]

Elizabethton School for Girls

Sometime during the 1830's efforts were begun to provide a limited amount of formal education for girls in and near Elizabethton.[25] The few references to the girls' school give a very incomplete picture of its activities.

William Gott, secretary of the board of trustees of the Elizabethton Female Seminary, announced that a public examination of the students would be held on Monday and Tuesday, October 7 and 8, 1839.[26] George Rich, teacher and president of the institution for the "last four sessions," had decided to remove to Kingsport to open a girls'

---

[24] Academy Papers. It is good to note that this was a common school and that the term was five months in length. The teacher was to receive all of $12.00 per month!

[25] The school probably began about 1835 or 1836. There was no school during the school year 1839-40 because of teacher shortage. Duffield's sessions lasted five months. Mrs. Furman, the new teacher in 1840, began the "eighth session." Elizabethton Whig, April 9, 1840.

[26] Ibid., September 12, 1839.

school there. The trustees "with a degree of regret" passed resolutions calling his departure "a public loss to the town and community."[27] Under his care and superintendency, they continued, the school had "acquired a standing among the finest seminaries of our state."

The November, 1839, session was delayed pending the arrival of a teacher, but during the winter months this new teacher, Mrs. Woods Furman, was secured. Finally, on March 16, 1841, the "eighth session" of the school began under her direction. Patrons of the school were assured they would "find in her a competent, as well as safe and faithful protector" of the morals of the girls.[28]

Terms of tuition were announced, reading, spelling, and writing, $6.00; arithmetic, geography, grammar, and composition, $8.00; natural, moral and mental philosophy, chemistry, astronomy, rhetoric, ancient and modern history, $10.00; music, $20.00; and painting, $10.00.[29]

Recollections written down about 1885 mention the fact that "A house which had been occupied by a common school and by a female academy was purchased and fitted up as a house of worship."[30] This, when referring as it did to the earliest Baptist church, helps one to

---

[27] Ibid., October 17, 1839.

[28] Ibid., April 9, 1840.

[29] Ibid., This curriculum compares very favorably with the studies made by Middlebrooks, op. cit. and Ward, op. cit. In fact terms were perhaps cheaper and board much more so. Most of the students who attended the school probably lived at their own homes and traveled back and forth to school.

[30] Goodspeed, op. cit., 911.

date the school inasmuch as this congregation was not organized until June, 1842. Again, James Adams was allowed $50.00 "to assist in building a bridge across Doe River near the _male_ Academy in Elizabethton."[31]

An old receipt gives light on how the institution was financed:

> Rec'd of Jacob Cameron twenty-two dollars and seventy-five cents the balance of his subscription towards Female Accadama [sic] this 14th March 1839.
>
> Jas. I. Tipton[32]

One is led to believe that this female school was a private, unincorporated school, which was rather common for the times.[33] The fact that Tipton as treasurer gave Cameron a receipt for the balance of "his subscription" seems to confirm this belief. This was the ordinary procedure followed by the subscription schools; one wonders if his subscription might not have been as much as $40.00.

The "Emme Female Academy" was incorporated by act of the legislature on February 3, 1850. The trustees appointed[34] suggest that this

---

[31] County Court Minutes, April, 1844, p. 220. The italics are those of the writer. Since the term "male Academy" is used in the official court records at that date, it seems reasonable to suppose it was so used to distinguish that institution from another, the "Female Academy or Seminary." Thus the Female Academy must have continued until after April, 1844.

[32] McCown Collection, Mrs. L. W. McCown, Johnson City.

[33] Ward, op. cit. found four kinds of academies: county, connected with state, receiving state funds as Duffield did; private incorporated academies; private, unincorporated academies; and church or fraternal schools. There is no record that the girls' school every received any state funds; no trace can be found of any incorporation before 1850; a study of the church records of all leading denominations gives no evidence of support; the Masonic order was weak; therefore, it must be concluded that the Elizabethton Female Seminary was a private, unincorporated school financed by subscriptions.

[34] A. W. Taylor, probably chairman, James I. Tipton, Peter Emmert, N. G. Taylor, M. N. Folsom, James Price, and Dr. Joseph Powell. Public Acts, 1850, Chapter CXXVII, 324.

may just be the incorporation of the school discussed above. This school was probably short-lived; of its operations nothing is known. Its excuse for existence was destroyed when the legislature passed in 1852 a law providing that any academy receiving state aid "must receive female as well as male pupils, and teach them in the several branches" of learning.[35] The fact that Mrs. Hover became a teacher at Duffield in 1853 suggests that the girls were admitted to that institution in that year.

Training Under Apprenticeship System

Not every child in the county had the opportunity to attend school at the academies in Elizabethton. What kind of education was furnished in the outlying parts of the county? Sometimes adverse circumstance prevented a child from receiving very much formal education. Such was the case with orphans and others of misfortune. For instance, two Howard children, orphaned at an early age, were "bound out" until they reached about the age of twenty-one. In this case Caroline Howard was to be given one year of schooling "between twelve and fifteen years of age." His master was George Brown who was to further furnish him two suits of clothing, "one fitting for the Lord's Day."[36]

---

[35] Public Acts, 1851-1852, Chapter CLXXXVI, 267.

[36] His brother, Isaac Howard, was bound out to George Lacy who agreed to give him a horse, saddle, and bridle, the total value of which was to be $100, and two suits of clothing when young Howard reached twenty-one. County Court Minutes, February 13, 1827.

In another way an occupation and practical on-the-job training was provided for children by the father's will. Before the death of William Jenkins, he provided that his son, Jessee, "be bound to the blacksmith trade," and that his son, Larkin, "be bound to the hatter's trade," and that his third son, Rowland, when "he is old enough to choose his trade," was to have a choice of being bound out "to joiners or wagon makers."[37]

The apprenticeship system in the various trades also may be considered as part of the educational program. There must have been many informal contracts between the parties; the details undoubtedly varied, but one contract is still in existence and is quite revealing. On August 6, 1836, young Allen A. Adams and Jacob B. Nelson entered a contract whereby Adams bound "himself to serve . . . . as an apprentice to the house carpenter's business for the term of three years."[38] Nelson agreed to give him "such instructions as may from time to time be necessary to aid him in learning the said business." He was further to pay him $50.00 each year, one-third in cash, and the remainder "in trade," and the young man was to have "one week's holiday at each Christmas." Boarding, lodging, washing and mending of clothes were to be furnished by Nelson who also agreed to pay "the boarding and tuition" of Adams for three months "at any school convenient to the

---

[37] Will of William Jenkins, dated September 7, 1806, 1800-1810 packet (County Court Clerk's office, Elizabethton).

[38] Nelson Papers.

parties"—such schooling to be after the "expiration of the three years service" or "earlier if agreed upon."

Common Schools in Carter County

In trying to reconstruct the course and progress of the common schools in Carter County, one is severely handicapped by the meagerness of details. If the bits of scattered information that are known are placed in the proper state-wide setting, then some picture of the common school system can be obtained.

During the years about the turn of the nineteenth century factors such as "ever-present danger of Indians, the sparseness of population, and the scarcity of money"[39] operated to lessen the influence of schools among the people of Tennessee, especially those away from the towns. Undoubtedly, however, many parents taught their children at least the basic fundamentals.

An act concerning education was passed by the state in 1815 which, unfortunately, caused a stigma to be attached to the common school. This act provided that a tax could be levied on property and polls to educate "those poor orphans who have no property to support and educate them, and whose fathers were killed or have died in the services of their country in the late war."[40] In the mind of too many

---

[39] A. P. Whitaker, "The Public School System of Tennessee 1834-1860," *Tennessee Historical Magazine* (The Tennessee Historical Society, Nashville) II, (March, 1916), 1.

[40] *Ibid.*, 2.

the state public school system and the "pauper school" system became one and the same thing. Many thought that to send their children to a "pauper school" was beneath their dignity and station in life. As a result many children did not attend any school and received little or no formal education, accounting in a great measure for the high illiteracy rating of the state in the census reports of 1840, 1850, and 1860.

In any discussion of the common school system in Tennessee it is necessary to mention a few of the essential facts concerning the state funds derived from the sale of public lands which came to the state as a result of the 1806 compact mentioned earlier. After 1823 when these lands were first put up for sale, the proceeds as well as rents from certain tracts of land became a perpetual school fund the interest of which was to be distributed to the counties to be used locally.[41] Only a pittance was received from this source and later the state added funds to this principal. In accordance with the common school law of 1830 these funds were divided among the counties in proportion to the number of their free white population. T. A. R. Nelson, clerk of the county school commissioners, reported that $4,418.02 was the amount "said to be due the county of Carter by the Cashier of the

---

[41] Hamer, op. cit., I, 353-356, for a more complete discussion. In 1836 the school fund was restored to the state and placed in the hands of a state superintendent ; in 1838 this amount was increased and deposited in the Bank of Tennessee which thereafter was required to set aside $100,000. each year for the common schools.

Bank of East Tennessee" in his letter of February 25, 1833, to David Nelson, chairman of the school commissioners.[42]

The 1830 law further provided that in each county at least five "discreet and intelligent citizens" were to be appointed county common school commissioners.[43] These were to have complete control of all money and property of the schools. They were to redistribute all common school money "according to children in each school district ages 5 to 15, including both sexes." The school district was roughly the area of a captain's militia district. Before the district could receive the money, there must be presented to the county school commissioners evidence that the district "has provided a comfortable school house." All money received had to be "honestly and faithfully applied to the support of a free school in the district." They were further empowered "to keep subscription paper and solicit and receive donations" to supplement the school fund. There was to be no distinction between the rich and poor. All children under the age of fifteen were

---

[42] Nelson Papers. From this source it is learned that David Nelson was chairman, T. A. R. Nelson was clerk, and that Benjamin White and John L. Williams were also county common school commissioners. David Nelson called a meeting of the commissioners to be held in the courthouse on June 29, 1834 "to apportion the school funds among the several school districts according to law." Washington Republican and Farmer's Journal (Jonesboro), June 21, 1834. It also appears from the Nelson report that an earlier clerk was Albert Moore since Nelson paid $25.50 to "G. Moore for Albert Moore . . . . for his services and for furnishing a book and postage." Nelson Papers, Report of June 29, 1833.

[43] Acts of Tennessee, 1829-30, Chapter CVII, pp. 140-141.

urged to attend. The good of the school required the school "to operate at the most leisure seasons of the year most convenient for children of the neighborhood."

In 1836 the school districts were made to coincide with the newly created civil districts. The interest manifested by the people in a school system is shown in the personnel elected in 1838 to serve as district school commissioners. Full returns are available for that election except for the fourth civil district and are given in the appendix.[44]

A report submitted to the state legislature by Mr. R. M. McEwen, state superintendent of public instruction, gives the scholastic population of the county for the year 1838-1839, broken down according to districts. The smallest number of pupils was located in the first district (the present Roan Mountain community) and the largest number was in the fifth district (Buffalo environs), followed closely by Elizabethton and surrounding community. The same report showed that $85.00 was collected by Nelson as tax on "tippling houses."[45]

District	Pupils	Amount	District	Pupils	Amount
1	88	$54.84	6	123	$ 76.64
2	59	36.77	7	206	128.37
3	85	52.97	8	152	94.72
4	121	75.40	9	140	87.24
5	213	132.73	10	170	105.94

[44] Infra., 197.

[45] Report of the Superintendent of Public Instruction (Nashville: J. Geo. Harris, 1839), 61, Appendix "A", 17.

It is interesting to compare the statistics of the four upper counties of the state at this early period. In 1841 the state distributed 64-11/16 cents per child.[46]

County	Pupils	Amount
Carter	1339	$ 866.67
Johnson	736	476.37
Washington	3024	1957.27
Sullivan	2737	1771.51

One cannot judge very clearly the effectiveness of this public school education, but if pupils attended school until they could read and write even a little, then the effort would seem to have been justified. Undoubtedly parents desired their children to progress further than they themselves had done. The growth of the public school system is noticeable when comparisons are made for several years.[47] Sometime after 1844, but before 1849, the number of school districts was increased to more than one per civil district. In 1849 there were twenty-nine school districts, and in 1858 there were thirty-three districts,[48] although the civil districts remained ten in number until 1856 when the eleventh was created.

A last glance at common school attendance in upper East Tennessee before the Civil War completely wrecked the school system shows attendance and state aid as follows:

---

[46] Ibid., 1841, pp. 20-21.

[47] A comparison of the pupil population for the years 1839, 1842, 1844, and 1850 is to be found in the appendix, infra., 198.

[48] County Court Minutes, August, 1849, p. 25; Report of the Superintendent of Public Instruction, 1859, pp. 168, 197.

County	Pupils	State Aid Received
Carter	2,621	$ 1,965.75
Johnson	1,554	1,165.50
Washington	4,910	3,682.50
Sullivan	4,362	3,271.50[49]

The population schedules of the 1850 census reports give us an identification of at least eight teachers,[50] all of whom were men.

This was the custom of the day everywhere except in the academies. Joseph Estabrook, president of East Tennessee University in 1838, deplored the fact that "none but men could teach . . . . and yet no man with any self-respect or ambition would teach, certainly for any length of time." He pointed out that "teaching in the common schools is an occupation very well suited to women's character and capacity."[51] By 1852 Tennessee by an act of the legislature had permitted female teachers to be employed and to be "paid in the same manner as other teachers."[52] This measure was designed to increase the effectiveness of the school system by making available additional teacher personnel.

---

[49] Ibid., 197, 206, 217, 219.

[50] 1. Samuel Miller, son of Mary Miller, age 24, lived in 5th district
2. James Hyder, age 21, son of Jonathan Hyder, lived in 5th district.
3. Alex. S. Y. Lusk, age 25, son of John L., lived in 5th district.
4. Tennessee H. Lusk, age 23, son of John L., lived in 5th district.
5. Nathaniel Buck, age 22, son of Ephraim Buck, lived in 5th district.
6. James F. Cass, age 42, a "schoolmaster," lived in 3rd district.
7. Eli Fletcher, age 32, lived in 8th district.
8. James E. Hyder, age 20, son of Jonathan H., lived in 7th district.
Seventh Census (1850), (microfilm).

[51] East Tennessee University Address, September 12, 1838, as quoted in Whitaker, loc. cit., 15.

[52] Acts of State of Tennessee, 1851-1852, Chapter CXXXIII, 188.

It is believed that Katy Collins, a sister to G. O. Collins, was one of the earliest lady teachers in the county school system.[53]

There were at least two sources of funds in the county for the common schools, namely, $2\frac{1}{2}$ cents per one hundred acres of school land and a share in the money derived from sale of liquor licenses. For the year 1832 the school system received $30.00, its share from licenses issued, and the small sum of 149.87\frac{1}{2}$ for the period 1825-28 and $323.57 for the period 1829-1832 from the school lands within the county.[54] The taxes for even this amount had not been properly collected or turned over, because William Gott, sheriff, made a note for the larger amount, while Nelson, as clerk, wrote the former sheriff in an effort to straighten out his collections "so our county, as early as practicable may begin to relize some of the benefits intended by the common school system."[55]

When common school funds received from the state were insufficient to pay the wages of the teacher, then the law provided that the district school commissioners had "power to collect the residue of such wages from parents . . . . who may have derived benefits from the school by

---

[53] Interview with "Aunt Nannie Smith," Elizabethton, February, 1950, who remembered her as a teacher "about the time of the Civil War. Earlier Elizabeth Singletary taught at Duffield.

[54] Nelson Papers, May and June, 1833.

[55] Ibid., May, 1833.

sending children thereto, and shall apportion the amount to be collected from each according to the number of children sent by each, and the length of time such children may have been at school."[56]

The same act provided that each child must furnish his "just proportion of fuel" except in the case of "indigent children" who could be excused by the district commissioners. More money was available after the passage of an act by the legislature in 1831 levying a $15.00 tax on retailers of liquors to "provide for the education of the children" within the school districts.[57] Later, in 1836, an act was passed which had as its purpose the recovery of all school money that had earlier been distributed to the counties.[58] In 1838 the state guaranteed one hundred thousand dollars annually to support the common schools to be distributed among the counties according to pupil population.[59] Several of the governors and legislatures talked about helping education in the state, but it was left to Andrew Johnson as governor to urge in 1853 that the legislature do something concrete to promote education in the state. In response the

---

[56] *Acts of State of Tennessee*, 1837-1838, Chapter CXLVIII, 212.

[57] *Public Acts of Tennessee*, 1831, Chapter LXXXXX, 101; T. A. R. Nelson, agent of the Superintendent of Public Instruction in Carter County, reported to his chief in 1839 that $85.00 was collected from the tax on retailers. *Report of Superintendent* 1839, Appendix "A," p. 17.

[58] On March 1, 1836, Carter County owed the state and was to return $4,476.51; by November 18, 1839, Nelson had paid into the Nashville office $5,924.96, and there was yet due $164.35. Ibid.

[59] Hamer, op. cit., I, 356.

legislature passed an act levying a tax of twenty-five cents on each poll and two and one-half cents on each hundred acres of land.[60] It further empowered the county courts to "levy and collect a tax on property, polls, and privileges not smaller than the state tax."[61] No trace of a county educational tax has been found in the Minutes of the County Court.

In the cases of two teachers we know something of the wages they received. In February, 1845, George Emmert, the trustee, was directed to pay to Joel Cooper the sum of $19.12½, "the amount due him for teaching school three months at Hughes school house in civil district No. 6."[62] In another instance Ben Walker in return for the schooling of his children, Joe and Nancy, paid his share to the teacher, Frank Hyder, at a school held in the Oak Grove-Powder Branch community, by giving him a cow.[63] "Uncle Joe" Walker also remembers that George Wright and George ("Dot") Williams were also his teachers "before the Civil War" and that parents often paid children's tuition by giving the teacher "corn and wheat" or other farm produce.

Since very early days there has been a school in the present Hunter community. Tradition is that about 1800 some of the people, chiefly the Carrigers, constructed an old log building for school

---

[60] Public Acts of Tennessee, 1853-1854, Chapter LXXI, 140.

[61] Ibid.

[62] Order signed by Isaac Tipton, Thomas Gourley, and one other commissioner who could only make his mark. In a very neat and legible script, Cooper endorsed the receipt and acknowledged payment on February 10, 1845. Found among County Court Minutes. (County Court Clerk's Office, Elizabethton).

[63] Interview with the student, Joe, now "Uncle Joe" Walker, over 100 years old, Valley Forge, Tennessee, December, 1949.

purposes. At any rate an agreement was reached February 4, 1826, among the residents of Watauga Valley to construct "a frame building twelve feet high 2 chimneys of stone or brick."[64] The school was to be located opposite Nave's mill on land donated by Godfrey Carriger, Jr. Twenty-one citizens were subscribers for the promotion of the worthwhile project.[65] About twenty years later the citizens on the south side of the Watauga River "agreed to build a schoolhouse in their neighborhood."[66] Daniel Stover, one of the subscribers, gave the land for the site, located at about the spot where the present Siam Baptist Church stands.

These two agreements are the only ones of which anything definite is known. Undoubtedly there are others. The population schedules of the 1840 census identified and located common schools in three places. One such school was housed in the "Buffalo Meeting House" (campus of present Milligan College); another was on "Buffalo Creek," probably farther up the creek, about the site of later Anderson School (Cave Springs); and the third was located in Elizabethton, probably outside the town.[67]

---

[64] County Court Minutes, November, 1827, 119; Deed Book J, 238 (Register of Deed's Office, Elizabethton).

[65] The trustees were Levi Nave, Caleb B. Cox, and Christian Carriger. Other subscribers were: Henry Nave, John Taylor, Mordecai Williams, David Nave, John T. Bowers, William Bishop, Andrew Emmert, William Taylor, Israel Cole, W. N. Hardin, William Allen, Christian C. Nave, Robert Blevins, John T. Allen, John Nav, Jr., Benjamin White, and Jeremiah Cannon. Ibid.

[66] This agreement was dated August 15, 1846, and the subscribers appointed Matthais VanHuss, Christian E. Carriger, and Daniel S. Bowers as trustees. Deed Book L, 43 (Register of Deed's Office, Elizabethton)

[67] Sixth Census (1840), (microfilm).

Indications are that private individuals in better circumstances than some of their neighbors constructed small schools on their lands for the benefit of their children and those of their friends. In the appendix the reader will find a listing of all the known schools in the county as well as the families whose children probably attended each particular school.[68] Many of these schools are remembered by the family name of the individual who gave the land or constructed the school such as the "Davis School," "Bell School," or the "Hughes School."

---

[68] Infra., 199-200.

CHAPTER FIVE

SLAVERY AND SECESSION IN CARTER COUNTY

Within the decade after the first settlements were made along the banks of the Watauga about 1769, some of the more prosperous pioneers brought with them their colored servants, probably the first ones being brought here from North Carolina or Virginia. In all probability during the Watauga Association days the colored man was already present in what is now Carter County.[1] A tax list of Washington County (North Carolina) for the year 1779 gives the names of the early slaveholders and their slave property. Ten of these early settlers whose names appear on the list can be identified as having owned property and having lived within the bounds of the county. This number included five who had previously signed the Watauga Petition to North Carolina asking for protection in 1776.[2] Undoubtedly the nearly fifty slaves owned by these ten men represent the accumulation of slaves brought into the new country during the years of the decade, 1769-79.

---

[1] Williams, *Revolutionary War*, 7.

[2] Those who had signed the Watauga Petition were Robert Lucas with four slaves shown on the list, Gideon Morris with 1; Joshua Houghton, Sr., 11; Andrew Greer, 2; Thomas Houghton, 3. The remaining five with their holdings were: Edmond Williams, 4; Joshua Houghton, Jr., 2; James Stuart and brother, Robert, 3; Henry Lile, 1; Mesach Hail, 1; William MacLin, 10; and Matthew Talbot (10 slaves in Virginia were to be sold to pay his taxes), Washington County List of Taxables, 1779, WPA Project No. 65-44-258 (County Court Clerk's Office, Jonesboro, Tennessee).

A few general remarks can be made concerning slaveholding during this early period. Only a few of the more wealthy family heads were owners of this kind of property. Certainly the average poor pioneer was without slaves when he arrived in the new country and without the supply of capital with which to purchase even a single slave. The work in which these early slaves participated was that of making extensive clearings and plantings and assisting in the erection of buildings. As usual there were also the general duties of the man-servant to his master and the maid-servant to her mistress.

An analysis of the tax listings returned by the various captains of Washington County militia companies for the years 1790, 1791, and 1795, together with the occasional mention of Negroes in a few wills of this period, give us some knowledge of who owned slaves and how many were of taxable age. A partial enumeration would certainly include these:

Name	1790 or 1791	1795
Jeremiah Bass	8	8
Pharoah Cobb	6	10
Andrew Greer, Sr.	2	3
Landon Carter	4	7
Edmond Williams	4	6
David Waggoner (Wagner)	2	3
Godfrey Carriger		2
Isaac Lincoln		3
Andrew Taylor	(1787 will mentions 4)	3
John Potter	(1790 will mentions "Negroes")	

---

[3]Ibid. Captain Nicholas Carriger's company included 9 slaveholders, total 39 slaves; Captain Joseph Ford's company, 2 with 7; Captain Nathaniel Taylor's 6 with 15; Captain Reuben Thornton's, 5 with 9. This makes a total of 22 slave owners with 70 slaves; however, some of those listed include names like Jeremiah Dungan and Garret Reasoner and others who appear to be more closely connected with the history of present Washington County. The Taylor will, May 22, 1787, and Potter will, November 18, 1789, are found in Will Book I, (Washington County Courthouse, Jonesboro, Tennessee).

A statistical picture of slavery in Carter County immediately after the formation of the county may be seen by studying the 1797 tax list.[4] A total of 27 citizens owned 80 slaves, and in accordance with the tax rate of that year, twenty-five cents on each slave, they would pay into the treasury twenty dollars. As seen on the accompanying table, the largest holders were, in order, Jeremiah Bass, Pharoah Cobb, Landon Carter, Richard White, and Nathaniel Taylor. It is interesting to compare this list with the four wealthiest men of the county, as shown by amount of tax to be paid and description of property:

    Landon Carter   tax to be paid, $17.12½; 10,600 acres of land, 1 white poll, 7 black polls, and 18 town lots.

    Nathaniel Taylor   tax to be paid, $5.25; 1,500 acres of land, 1 white poll, 5 black polls, 1 stud horse.

    Pharoah Cobb   tax to be paid, $4.92; 640 acres of land, 1 white poll, 8 black polls, 1 stud horse.

    Isaac Lincoln   tax to be paid, $4.15; 820 acres of land, 1 white poll, 4 black polls, 1 stud horse.

---

[4] Interesting also is the List of Taxable Property and Tax for Carter County for the years 1796, 1798, and 1799. A compilation of these four lists would be an invaluable aid to those interested in genealogical studies. Tenn. Archives.

SLAVE OWNERS AND NUMBER OF SLAVES OWNED BY EACH AS
FOUND ON THE 1797 COUNTY TAX LIST

William Boyd	2	William Davis	1
Jeremiah Bass	9	James Eden, Sr.	1
Julius Conner	3	Andrew Greer, Sr.	3
Pharaoh Cobb	8	Alexander Greer	3
Josiah Clark	1	William Griffin	2
Godfrey Carriger, Sr.	2	Isaac Lincoln	4
Abraham Cox	1	John Peoples	1
John Carter	2	Nathaniel Taylor	5
Landon Carter	7	Jonathan Tipton, Jr.	1
Benjamin Cutbirth, Sr.	1	Joseph Tipton	1
Jesse Whitson	3	Samuel Tipton	3
Archibald Williams	1	Lucretia Williams	3
Richard White	6	David Wagner	4
Matthias Wagner	2		

Of the 460 slaves indicated on the 1830 census reports[5] only 171 are listed for tax purposes. From this we infer that more than half of those listed as slaves were not of taxable age--either under ten years of age or over fifty. A study of the revenue docket kept by George Williams, the county court clerk for many years, reveals the number of slaves listed for the years from 1827 through 1835, showing a low of 157 in 1834 and a high of 218 in the following year, 1835.[6]

---

[5]For a statistical table of the number of Negroes, free and slave, for the period 1800-1860, see appendix, infra., 201.

[6]A sampling of the number of slaves listed for tax purposes gives this information:

1796	80	1829	176	1834	157
1799	93	1830	171	1835	218
1813	155	1831	172	1860	158
1827	178	1832	187	1861	178
1828	168	1833	198		

It is to be regretted that such information is not available for all years. Tax Lists and State Tax Certifications, Tenn. Archives, Nashville; Revenue Docket (Carter County) 1826-1847, 6 et passim and Tax Lists for 1860 and 1861 (County Court Clerk's Office, Elizabethton).

A governmental theory of the day was that all property including slaves should be taxed and our early state constitutions so provided. Thus the slaveowner was frequently "hit hard" by taxes on his slave property. In 1796 a twenty-five cent tax was levied on each slave and by 1804 the tax was seventy-five cents. Later it was reduced to 62½ cents for the year 1820, then to 50 cents in 1830, but the rate was increased to 87½ for the years 1827, 1828, and 1831. By the next year, 1832, it had reached an all-time high of a $1.00 per slave,[7] with specific assessments as follows: 25 cents for the contingent fund (operating expenses), 25 cents as a poor tax, 37½ cents to build a new jail, and 12½ listed as an additional tax to cover various appropriations.

Concerning the sale and transfer of slaves in this county, the writer has reached certain tentative and general conclusions after an extensive analysis of bills of sale covering such transactions as recorded in the Register's Office, Elizabethton.[8] In the first place, the selling price of slaves in most cases depended upon age, physical conditions, special abilities, and the like. A young boy or girl, age ranging from 11 or 12 up to 17 or 20, would bring from about three to five hundred dollars. A few examples:

```
1807   Mary Greer to A. M. Carter, a girl, age 16, $463.00
1807   Godfrey Carriger to John Carriger, a boy, 15, $400.00
1808   Johnston Hampton to Joseph Vaught, a girl, $350.00
1809   James S. Johnson to A. M. Carter, a mulatto boy, 17, $400.00
1821   Thomas D. Love to James P. Taylor, a girl, age 13, $400.00
1824   William B. Carter to James P. Taylor, a girl, age 14, $400.00
1827   Valentine Bowers to Godfrey Nave, a boy, age 12, $350.00
```

---

[7]From a study of various tax rates levied for the years mentioned. County Court minutes.

[8]Information and samples given are derived from a careful study of more than 150 bills of sale. Deed Books A through N, 1796-1861.

If, however, the slave had special abilities, he then commanded a much higher price. For instance, these four transactions are of interest:

1808 A. M. Carter to Elihue Embree, a Negro named Isaac, age 21, $1,000 (probably an iron worker since both men are known to have been connected with mine operations).

1822 Gowen and John Patterson to William B. Carter, a Negro man named Charles, age 27, $1,000 (probably iron worker).

1824 Wm. B. Carter to James P. Taylor, a Negro named Henry, $600, originally purchased from Matthias Wagner.

1825 Gowen Patterson to James I. Tipton, a Negro named Charles, a hammer man by trade, $900.

Secondly, there seems to have been an obvious attempt to keep together members of a Negro family, at least the mother and her children, whenever this could possibly be accomplished. There seems to be on record very few cases where the identify of the father is made known.[9] Family relationships in these sales were not severed:

1808 Samuel English (Burke County, N. C.) to Nathaniel Taylor, family of three: Ester, 23, Luvice, $3\frac{1}{2}$, and Hampton, 2, $665.

1810 John McAllister (Jonesboro) to Godfrey Carriger, Sr., family of six: Isaac, a mulatto, 24; Nancy, 26; Frances, a mulatto, 10; William, 8; Abigail, 5; and Sophia about 2, $1530.32 (originally sold to McAllister by Elihue Embree).

1816 Mary Lincoln (widow of Isaac Lincoln) to Godfrey Carriger, Sr., a family of three: Violet, a mulatto, 23; Nathaniel, 3, and Jessee, 1, $900.

---

[9] "Aunt Jo" Taylor, Church Street, Elizabethton, now about 96, remembers well her slave days. She was 11 years old when the Civil War ended. In an interview with the writer on June 10, 1950, she told how slave took the name of his mother. Her own mother, Tina by name, was born in Africa and apparently took the name of Taylor when she was purchased at Jonesboro by George and William Taylor.

1822 Jacob Smith to Daniel Smith, family of four; Rubin, 50; Susan, 24; Children, Muit, 6; and James, 3, $1300.

1828 John Cocke (Grainger County, Tennessee) to Christian Carriger, family of three: Dolly, 45; Bleavins, a mulatto, 3; Cynthia, a mulatto, $500.

Numerous examples can be cited where the mother and one child were sold together, usually the child being very young. In other cases, it appears that a brother and sister were sold together. In still another way, members of a slave family were kept in close contact with each other through the operation of bills of sale between the members of the master's family or through the operation of the master's will bequeathing the members of a slave family to various children in the master's family.

Thirdly, there is little evidence to indicate that a wide-spread traffic in slaves existed. Principally accounting for the maintenance and slight increase in the Negro population from decade to decade was the natural increase among the slaves. Not uncommon was the Negro mother of sixteen or thereabouts and not surprising was it to find a Negro mother bringing into this world children when she herself had passed the 40 or 45 year mark. The Negro family was large.[10] A fact generally true of white families as well.

The most frequent transactions on record are those between citizens of Carter County. Next in frequency are sales involving the

---

[10] "Aunt Jo," referred to in the preceding footnote, is the youngest of ten children born to slave Tina Taylor.

transfer of Negroes from adjoining Sullivan and Washington counties. A few slaves were brought in from outside the state, from nearby North Carolina or Virginia. There is some evidence to substantiate the claim that big mine operators imported slave labor.[11] In a few instances slaves were sold to people outside the state, usually residents of North Carolina.

As was often the custom, some slaveowners of the county provided that upon their death or the death of another person, usually the widow or some other close member of the family, some slave or a number of slaves were to be emancipated. One such case is to be found in the example of Edy Carter, faithful slave of Elizabeth Carter, the wife of Landon Carter. After the death of widow Elizabeth, which occurred February 27, 1842, at the home of her daughter, Mrs. Sallie Stewart Brewer, it was discovered in her will, dated March 22, 1841, that she had provided that Edy Carter should be set free.[12]

The executors of this will, Alfred M. Carter, and A. W. Taylor, appeared before the county court and asked that Edy be freed in accordance with the terms of the will and the laws of the state.

---

[11] Two citizens of South Carolina, Joseph Nethy in 1816 and John Smyth of Charleston in 1813, sold slaves to Nathaniel Taylor. Deed Book C, 514-515. There were several transfers of slaves between the Carters, Taylors, and O'Briens, all known to have engaged in the iron industry. Judge Williams, in his biographical sketch, <u>Brigadier-General Nathaniel Taylor</u> (Johnson City: The Watauga Press, 1940), p. 12, stated, "He owned, also, many slaves. His books of account show that for one gang of slaves he paid $12,000; these were imported from Africa to the port of Charleston, South Carolina. Slaves were needed to work on his plantation and in his iron works."

[12] Will on file County Court Clerk's Office, Elizabethton. More than 16 Negroes are listed in her will, 15 of them by name, the others as "children."

Thereupon in accordance with existing law the court issued an order stating that "the said Negro woman be emancipated and be henceforth entitled to all the rights and privileges of a free woman of color agreeably /sic/ to the laws of the land."[13] She then petitioned the court that she be allowed to remain in the county, giving as her reasons that she had lived in the county "for many years," and "her children mostly reside here and the children and friends of her old mistress to whom in distress she would look for friendship."[14] Finding her a "woman of good character," the court granted her request when George Duffield and Alfred W. Taylor put up a $500 bond as her security.

Two other examples will be cited. In his will, dated October 15, 1814, Alexander Doran provided that his "negro woman Cet Lallow" was "to be set free" upon the death of her mistress,[15] and Jessee Humphreys provided that his three Negroes, Glascow, Moriah, and Delph, as well as their mother, Lucy, should be "liberated" unless his wife survived him.[16]

---

[13] County Court Minutes, January, 1843, p. 152.

[14] Unable to write her name, she made her mark on the petition submitted. Ibid., 153.

[15] Will on file County Court Clerk's office, Elizabethton, 1810-1820 packet.

[16] Will dated October 9, 1818, ibid. Later his widow, Mary Humphreys, petitioned the state legislature to allow her to free these three and their mother. She further asked that they be allowed to remain in the county because she did not have "the means to send to the colony of Liberia." She related that it would be a "source of grief to her in her dying hour to think of those unfortunate Human beings, (who had attended upon their deceas'd master with so much affection during his many years and also on your memoralist to the present time with equal affection and kindness) being left slaves for life with their posterity." September 3, 1832, Tenn. Archives.

The increase in the feeling that slaves should be set free is found in another example from the court records. This time Isaac Anderson asked the court to free two slaves, Harry and his wife Nelly, "because they have been to him faithful and dutiful servants for many years having contributed greatly to the raising of the petitioner from infancy and because he believes that their happiness and comfort would be promoted by it." This couple likewise petitioned the court to remain in the county, stating that they had lived there "for the last 35 years" and that "all their white and black friends are here."[17]

For the most part Carter County slaveowners looked upon their Negroes with much kindness and with real concern for their well-being. The master and his family regarded them as part of the family, and, indeed, many of the slaves did have the same last name as their master. One slaveowner in Elizabethton felt this way about his Negroes. After listing the members of his immediate family, giving the usual information found in a family Bible, Jacob Cameron then listed with as much detail the descendants of Jane Cameron, black woman.[18]

---

[17] Isaac Anderson, Clayton Reeve, and George W. Peoples posted a $1,000 security bond for the couple. County Court Minutes, January, 1844, pp. 207-210.

[18] Story related to the writer by Mrs. L. W. McCown of Johnson City. The original Jacob Cameron Bible is now in possession of Mrs. J. R. Boring, Elizabethton.

The slave usually responded in terms of affection toward his master and his family. Not uncommon were "marster," "the missus," "uncle," "aunt," and "cousin." Many Negroes seem to have felt a sense of pride in their master's family and its success. The writer has noticed this sense of pride especially manifested by the Taylor slaves and has heard stories of how the Carter slaves prided themselves on the Carter family traditions and records. A good indication of how the slave regarded the master and his family is to be found in the numbers of Negroes who remained with their masters' families after emancipation.[19] Many of the Negroes were given the choice of remaining on with the family, working for wages, instead of being slaves.

Doctor Abraham Jobe, some thirty years after the close of the Civil War, in writing his Memoirs or Autobiography gives us the contents of a discussion that he had with his two slaves who were being set free. It gives us a picture of how he must have treated his slaves before the war. He wrote:

> I will promise to treat you just as I have always treated you. I will clothe you and feed you, and you may work just as you please, with no task master over you—just as you know you always have done ever since you lived with me, and be cared for, and nursed when Sick, the same as any of the balance of my family—the Same as I always treated you, not even giving you a cross word.[20]

---

[19] Moriah Howard lived on with the Major H. M. Folsom family until her death about 1922. "Aunt Jo" Taylor told the writer that she, some of her brothers and sisters, and her mother remained with the Taylors until the death of her "missus," Mary, wife of Alfred W. Taylor.

[20] Unpublished manuscript now in possession of Mrs. L. W. McCown, Johnson City. There is no evidence or reason to believe that Dr. Jobe did not say substantially what is here quoted as he later wrote it. One of his slaves chose to leave, but the other one, Tilda, remained with the family until her death, May 3, 1891 (p. 191).

When "Aunt Jo," the former slave, was questioned about whether her master and family were good to her, she enthusiastically and warm-heartedly related how they "never struck me a lick in my life," always "gave us plenty to eat," "taught us to do everything we knew how to do," including "reading and writing."[21]

Governor Bob Taylor, one of the two famous Taylor brothers of Carter County's famed Happy Valley, in one of his celebrated lectures, "Dixie," told of the relationship between master and slave. "The outside world can never know the true relation of master and slave," he informed his audience and then continued:

> The master was kind to his slaves, and history does record such devotion as that which was exhibited by the slave himself when he stood guard by the door at night and worked in the field by day to protect and feed the white women and children of the South while his master was far away on the battle field, fighting for the perpetuation of slavery.[22]

Governor Taylor, looking into the future and evaluating the work of the Negro, waxed oratorical as he concluded:

---

[21] Interview with the writer, June 10, 1950. When questioned if she had ever heard of any Carter County family which was "mean" to its slaves, she rather hesitatingly replied that she had heard that "a Thomas family" had been accused of that charge. Only one other Carter County family has come in for censure along this line. The Baker family of Limestone Cove is said to have been "mean" to their slaves. Mrs. Bob Patton, Milligan College, told the writer that she distinctly remembers her mother, Mrs. Ezekiel Birchfield, tell how the Baker slaves were mistreated (interview, May, 1950). Contrary to the generally accepted thought that slaveowners were guilty of mistreating their slaves, those who owned slaves in Carter County regarded them almost as members of the family. Other stories have been told the writer which confirm this point.

[22] Augsburg, op. cit., 139 ff.

>   The time will come when the South will build a
> monument to the old-time black man-servant for his fidelity
> and devotion to his master, and to the old-time black
> mammy for the lullabies she has sung.[23]

There is ample evidence to show that the Negro was received into the various church groups with the possible exception of the Elizabethton Presbyterian. From as early as about 1797 to as late as February 10, 1854, the Sinking Creek Baptist Church had colored members and they are mentioned in the records. At the latter date William Jobe, a man of color, was given permission to "exercise his gift in public," thus being permitted to preach.[24] Eleven colored members were reported by the Watauga Baptist Church in 1853.[25]

A colored woman, Edy Carter, emancipated by the will of Elizabeth Carter in 1842, became one of the charter members of the

---

[23]Ibid., 143. Speaking of the colored folk in general throughout the whole of the Confederacy, one writer gave a contrast, more realistic and undoubtedly closer to the truth: "They were not the docile "Old Kentucky Home" type of subservients that romancers have depicted them to be. Most of them idealized freedom and grasped it with alacrity when Yankee soldiers brought it within convenient reach. While the slaves waited for emancipation, they raised foodstuffs for civilians and soldiers, ran spinning wheels and looms on the plantations, worked in factories and mines, built fortifications, and served as nurses, cooks, and personal servants in the Southern army. Their good humor buoyed the spirits of white associates both at home and on the firing line. Their contribution to the Southern cause was enormous." Bell I. Wiley, The Plain People of the Confederacy (Baton Route: Louisiana State University Press, 1943), viii.

[24]MSCBC, 203.

[25]MHBA, 1853; later in 1856 the church reported 12 colored members, but by 1861 there were only 9 active.

Elizabethton Baptist Church in April, 1842. It is also quite possible that Fanny Renfro, colored, can also lay claim to being another charter member of that first Baptist Church in Elizabethton. She was granted a letter of dismissal from the church on September 24, 1842. Them, Matilda, a colored woman of Dr. Jobe's, was received by letter into the church on October 8, 1853. From the Watauga congregation Sally Bowers transferred her membership to the Elizabethton church in the year 1858.[26]

The Methodist and the Christian congregations throughout the county likewise included colored members among their numbers. In 1835 the Elizabethton Methodist Circuit reported to the Holston Methodist Conference a total of fourteen Negro members.[27] Later in 1848 the Methodists reported for Elizabethton and the Johnson Mission a total of forty-four Negro members, while the Watauga Mission was carrying seven Negroes on its membership roll.[28]

Not only were the colored folk received into the Buffalo Christian Church, but they contributed their share to the financing of church

---

[26] It is the conviction of the writer, after living all his years in Carter County, that some good "church" people today would certainly not be as tolerant and as respectful toward the colored people as were their forefathers a century ago. Incidents referred to with respect to the Elizabethton Baptist Church are cited from Minutes of that organization, passim.

[27] Price, op. cit., III, 293.

[28] Early, op. cit., I, 167 and 673 ff.

activities. One of the colored women of the congregation was "Aunt Mary Bob," belonging to James I. Tipton, an early Christian church minister.[29] Preacher Tipton is recorded as giving one dollar on November 21, 1835, and his slave woman gave twelve and one-half cents. Three other times her name appears on the contributor's list, one time for twenty-five cents. Other colored members of the church were Dinah Peoples who gave five cents, the "James I. Tipton colored man," who gave twelve and one-half cents, and a "Thomas woman slave," who also gave twelve and one-half cents.[30]

During the years just preceding 1861 the people of Carter County were called upon to answer the question facing the whole country. How would they stand upon the questions threatening to disrupt the American Union? Was slavery as that "peculiar institution of the South" and the theory behind state's right sufficient to cause them to sever the ties with our northern friends? To these questions the citizens of Carter were not slow to reply.

In fact the congressional election of 1859 was one of the most interesting ever waged in the first district. Thomas A. R. Nelson, old time Whig and more recently termed an American by political preference,

---

[29] Family tradition repeated to the writer by Mrs. L. W. McCown of Johnson City, is that "Aunt Mary Bob," as she was affectionately known, lived in a little house of her own in the James I. Tipton yard. She served him faithfully for many years as cook, going with him even on his preaching tours.

[30] Professor Sam Hyder Collection.

was stumping the district paired against that polished and powerful orator, Landon C. Haynes, who later was to be elected as one of Tennessee's senators to the Confederate Congress. Haynes, of course, was the Democrat making an all out effort to stem the Union sentiment in the county. With the aid of friends in Carter, he polled one of the largest Democratic votes up to that time. A comparison of the votes for the upper counties reveals:

	Carter	Johnson	Washington	Sullivan
Nelson	812	547	542	996
Haynes	342	218	1589	1335[26]

When one remembers that Stoney Creek, comprising the ninth and tenth civil districts, was largely an agricultural and mine works section, one can see significance in H. M. Folsom's letter to the victorious Nelson. He reported that "your main and principle loss was on Stoney Creek and you will be able to account for that when you remember that Rueben Brooks lives there." He added his congratulations on his victory over the "Cicero of America."[27] Three times defeated by the Democrats during the fifties for the same congressional seat, N. G. Taylor sent his best wishes on the occasion, stating that "Colonel Hayne /sic/ is my brother-in-law and esteemed personal friend . . . . /I/ sympathize with him and am sorry for him personally in his defeat." However, Taylor rejoiced that in the person of Nelson the

---

[26] Official county returns sent to the Governor, Tenn. Archives.

[27] From Elizabethton, August 8, 1859, Nelson Papers.

"1st Dist. has been redeemed from the domination of the corrupt democracy."[28] So ended round one.

In the 1860 presidential election the Republican ticket was not even run in Carter or the state of Tennessee for that matter. With N. G. Taylor touring the state and using his influence in the county as a Bell elector, the returns showed interesting results indicating how the county was beginning to feel about the deep-seated question of secession which by this time had absorbed and overshadowed the slavery question. Comparing the returns for Carter with her neighboring counties, one finds this situation:

Candidates	Carter	Johnson	Sullivan	Washington
Douglas	15	4	69	62
Breckinridge	205	140	1517	1331
Bell	859	508	538	967 [29]

After the general elections of 1860 in which the Republican Lincoln was elected president, and following the secession of South Carolina and some of the other lower southern states, the Tennessee legislature called upon the citizens of the state to vote in an election the results of which would determine whether the State would then leave the Union. N. G. Taylor again gave a picture of the sentiment in the county. In another letter to Nelson he informed him that Andrew Johnson's recent speech for the Union cause in the Senate was "applauded by the People of all parties here and will do much good." He then went on to

---

[28] Ibid., from Buffalo Mill, August 10, 1859.

[29] Goodspeed, op. cit., 358-359.

say that "Tennessee is for the Union as long as it can be honorably maintained in other words as long as it lasts."[30] Although Johnson was a Democrat and the county was predominately Whig in sentiment, he had considerable influence on opinion especially after his determined stand for the cause of the Union. His influence was increased because his son-in-law, Daniel Stover, a man of some means, lived in Carter in the Watauga Valley.[31]

The results of the election held on the 9th of February, 1861, indicated an overwhelming vote in favor of remaining with the Union and against the calling of a convention to consider the matter of secession. Again comparing the votes of the upper counties, one finds:

County	For Convention (Favor Secession)	Against Convention (Favor Remaining Union)
Carter	55	1055
Sullivan	1180	734
Washington	891	1353[32]

Referring to Tennessee history of that period, it will be remembered that Governor Isham G. Harris and other prominent leaders were in favor of secession and in sympathy with the Confederate cause. After the

---

[30] January 3, 1861, Nelson Papers.

[31] It will be remembered that President Andrew Johnson died in Carter County at the home of his daughter, Mrs. Daniel Stover, on July 31, 1875.

[32] Knoxville Whig, February 16, 1861. In several of issues following, Brownlow published the East Tennessee results with stirring editorials in favor of the Union. W. G. Brownlow in his Sketches of the Rise, Progress, and Decline of Secession (Philadelphia: George W. Childs, 1862), 220. The writer could not find the returns for Johnson County, but it is known that they voted overwhelmingly in favor of the Union and against the proposed Convention.

fall of Fort Sumter on April 14, 1861, President Lincoln issued the call for volunteers to be used against the Confederacy. Harris refused to send Tennessee's quota and immediately called a special session of the legislature. At that session the legislation provided that another election be held on the 8th of June following. The people of the state were to decide on the question of "Separation" or "No Separation" from the Union and "Representation" or "No Representation" in the Confederate States Congress.

Available is a letter representing the secessionist point of view giving an idea of how and why Carter County would vote in the approaching election. From Jonesboro, on May 17, 1861, Mr. A. E. Jackson wrote Colonel Landon C. Haynes:

> You may expect to hear a poor account from Carter in the coming election, they will no doubt bully southern rights voters at the polls and will force into the ranks of the opposition many who would otherwise vote for sustaining the action of the legislature—They have forced Burrow to resign the clerkship of the circuit court and are threatening violence to the open secessionists in the country—N. G. T. /Taylor/ is following in the wake of Johnson and Nelson and has pledged himself to remove to Kentucky if Tennessee goes out of the Union.33

The people of Carter, and in fact practically all East Tennessee, did not wait until the June 8 election to be heard. They were called together at Knoxville on May 30 and 31 in a convention to consider what action to further the cause of the Union could be taken. Representing Carter at the convention were Abraham Tipton, Charles P. Toncray, Daniel L. Stover, John W. Cameron, and

---

33 Nelson Papers.

J. P. T. Carter.³⁴ The convention was adjourned to meet after the coming election at Greeneville on June 17.

The people of Carter turned out stronger for the Union in this next election than in February. The results for the four counties again show how decidedly Carter and Johnson were for the Union cause and the relative strength of secession in Washington and Sullivan counties.

	Separation	No Separation	Representation	No Representation
Carter	86	1343	86	1343
Johnson	111	787	111	786
Sullivan	1586	627	1576	637
Washington	1022	1445	1016	1444³⁵

At the Greeneville Convention the county was represented by twenty-two delegates who joined in with their associates from all over East Tennessee in a memorial to the state legislature asking the consent for "the counties composing East Tennessee and such other counties in Middle Tennessee as desire to Co-operate with them, may form and erect a separate State."³⁶

But the die was cast. Tennessee seceded from the Union and became officially a member of the Confederate States of America.³⁷

---

³⁴Proceedings of the East Tennessee Convention (Knoxville: H. Barry's Book & Job Office, 1861), 6 et passim.

³⁵Knoxville Whig, June 15, 1861; Goodspeed, op. cit., 532-533.

³⁶Proceedings of the East Tennessee Convention, 7. Carter's delegates included A. Tipton, Wm. Marsh, L. Slagle, J. Emmert, T. M. Hilton, L. Carter, W. B. Carter, J. Perry, V. Singletary, B. M. G. O'Brien, Robert Williams, C. Wilcox, H. Slagle, D. Stover, J. Hendrickson, J. G. Lewis, W. J. Crutcher, S. P. Angel, J. L. Bradley, C. P. Toncray, John M. Smith, and H. C. Smith. Also see Samuel W. Scott and Samuel Angel, History of the 13th Regiment (Philadelphia: P. W. Ziegler & Co., 1903), 44. With possibly one or two exceptions, none of the delegates were owners of slaves.

³⁷Technically Tennessee did not "secede" from the Union; she "declared her independence" and then joined the Confederate States of America.

However, that did not make Carter County forget its first loyalty. Her citizens were now ready to sacrifice all for the sake of freedom. A Jonesboro paper informed its readers that "A majority of the people of Carter County are for adhering to the old flag--the stars and stripes --until the last."[38]

The August elections came and the people showed their defiance of the Confederate authorities by holding their regular congressional elections. They cast 1229 votes for T. A. R. Nelson, candidate for the United States Congress, while Joseph B. Heiskell received only 81 votes for the Confederate Congress.[39]

Thus it can be seen that the great majority of Carter County citizens, both men and women, openly proclaimed their allegiance to the national Union.[40] They could say with Dr. Abraham Jobe that they

---

[38] The Express, Jonesboro, Tenn., July 5, 1861, clipping in Nelson Scrapbooks (McClung Collection, Lawson McGhee Library, Knoxville).

[39] James L. Bradley, County Court Clerk, in his certification to Nelson, dated August 9, 1861. Callaway Elrod of Johnson County certified that Nelson received 1,129 votes while Heiskell received only 109 votes in that county. Nelson Papers.

[40] One writer in his analysis of the reasons why East Tennessee was overwhelmingly Unionist in their sentiment concluded these as contributing reasons. In most instances they appear to be reasonable and valid as far as Carter County was concerned. Some of his reasons were: "they had long been conscious of a sectional difference from the other parts of the state . . . . the tide of secession sentiment . . . . reached them too late to work its full effects . . . . lack of wealth made them feel they would have no place among a slaveholding aristocracy . . . . /the majority/ harbored a real political hatred for the Democratic party. . . . so closely connected with the secession movement that East Tennesseans considered secession a party affair . . . . powerful propaganda and in some cases too intimidation on the part of the Union leaders of the section . . . . leaders and followers alike dreaded war." Verton M. Queener, "East Tennessee Sentiment and the Secession Movement, November; 1860 - June, 1861." East Tennessee Historical Society's Publications, No. 20 (1948), 82-83.

"espoused the cause of the Union very early, when the war clouds first began to rise," and that "although born and reared in the South," they "could see nothing but disaster in Secession."[41]

---

[41] Dr. Jobe's Autobiography. Just to complete the story the writer here inserts the names of some of the more prominent people of the county who were secessionists in their thinking and actions: H. M. and G. W. Folsom, A. W. and N. M. Taylor, Robert Love, William J. Stover, W. C. Emmert, Reuben Brooks, Christian Crowe, Isaac L., Henry C. and Jacob Nave, Sanford Jenkins, and John S. Thomas. Scott and Angel, op. cit., 365 et passim. Many of these, if not nearly all, were slaveowners or those who believed in slaveholding. Infra., 202-206.

CHAPTER SIX

SUMMARY

The Carter County area was the very center of settlement during the Watauga Association period. The land was the scene of an early free government in American and later of important Indian negotiations. It was from Sycamore Shoals that the westerners marched to defeat the British at King's Mountain. From its bounds have gone many settlers to the other parts of Tennessee and the old Southwest. As a part of Washington County and later Wayne County under the State of Franklin, the growth and progress of the county was steady.

In 1796 the county was created and named in honor of Landon Carter. The influence of the Carters, Tiptons, Taylors, and Williamses was very pronounced in the early history of the county. When repeated efforts to move the county seat to a more centrally located site failed, the citizens of the northern and eastern part petitioned the state legislature for creation of a separate county which was named in honor of Thomas Johnson. More democratic government came to the county as a result of the Tennessee Constitution of 1834. The captain's militia company was replaced by the civil district about 1836 as the smallest governmental unit. The county left the Jacksonian party and became a Whig stronghold in 1836 chiefly because of opposition to certain Jacksonian policies, and the influence of Brownlow's Whig which had its beginnings in Elizabethton. The Whig Party, under a variety of names, continued to carry the county vote, and the county was predominately against secession at the outbreak of the Civil War.

Religion has played an important part in the history of the county. The Baptists were the first to organize and quickly spread over most of the county. One of their churches, Sinking Creek, claims to be the oldest church in Tennessee. The Presbyterians, very active in surrounding areas, quite early were nosed out of second place in importance by the Methodists who spread from the Elizabethton circuit headquarters. A few congregations, known locally as Christian churches, were making progress by the beginning of the Civil War.

The earliest well-to-do families sent their children away to school. In 1806 Duffield Academy, named in honor of George Duffield, was established and was used as both a school and church. This first school was financed by state aid and funds from tuition and donations. Until the time of the Civil War Duffield Academy compared favorably with other county academies. By about 1836 a girls' female seminary was established in Elizabethton, but by 1852 girls were admitted to Duffield Academy. In the early 1830's a county common school system was in existence, and it continued to improve with the passing of the years. Before the Civil War wrecked the school system, good attendance and fair results were being achieved.

Negro slaves were present in the Carter County area in the early days of the Watauga Association. A few old tax lists give information as to owners and their holdings. Bills of sale, the county tax rate, and population schedules of census reports give a continuing look at slavery. By legal action some slaves were emancipated, but there was never more than five hundred slaves in the county. Contrary to popular opinion, slaveowners were good to their slaves; slaves were also admitted to church membership. The great majority of the citizens were actively unionist in their sentiment. Less than ninety citizens of the county voted for secession in 1861.

BIBLIOGRAPHY

PRIMARY SOURCES

Carter County Records

1. County Court Minutes, 1804-1806; 1819-1820; 1826-1833; 1836-1840; 1841-1861. Office of County Court Clerk, Elizabethton.

2. Deeds and Bills of Sale, 1796-1861, Deed Books A Through N. Office of the Register of Deeds, Elizabethton.

3. Account Book, 1796-1835. County Court Clerk's Office.

4. Revenue Docket, 1826-1847; 1853-1861. County Court Clerk's Office.

5. Original Manuscript Wills, 1796-1860. County Court Clerk's Office.

Washington County Records

1. Deeds, 1782-1795, Vol. I-VII. Register of Deeds Office, Jonesboro.

2. Wills, Book I. County Court Clerk's Office, Jonesboro.

Church Minutes

1. Minutes of the Sinking Creek Baptist Church, 1794-1861. Now in possession of Mr. Fred Hinkle, King Springs Road, Johnson City, Tennessee.

2. Minutes of the Elizabethton Baptist Church (First), 1842-1861. Now in possession of Mr. Wiley Jenkins, Race Street, Elizabethton.

3. Minutes of the Presbyterian Church (First), 1833-1861. Now in possession of Mr. Steve Burnett, Elizabethton.

4. Minutes of the Holston Baptist Association, I, 1786-1850; II, 1850-1865. Now in possession of Mrs. B. D. Akard, Fairview Street, Johnson City. Minutes were published in pamphlet form after 1852 at following places: 1852 and 1853, Greeneville Spy Office; 1854 Jonesborough L. Gifford and Co.; 1855 (probably Jonesborough); 1856, Abingdon Virginian Office; 1857 and 1858, Knoxville, Barry's Job and Book Office, 1859-1861, Jonesborough, Wm. A. Sparks and Co.

5. Minutes of the Annual Conferences Methodist Episcopal Church, I, 1773-1828; II, 1829-1839; III, 1840-1845.

6. Minutes of the Annual Conferences Methodist Episcopal Church South, I, 1845-1857; II, 1857-1865.

Collections

1. Nelson Papers, 1828-1861. Lawson-McGhee Library, Knoxville.

2. McClung Collection. Lawson-McGhee Library.

3. Mrs. L. W. McCown Collection. Johnson City.

4. Fred Hinkle Collection. Kings Spring Road, Johnson City.

5. Vaught-Carriger Collection. Mrs. W. M. (Carriger) Vaught, Elizabethton.

6. Sam Hyder Collection. Milligan College, Tennessee.

7. Academy Papers Collection. Register of Deeds Office, Elizabethton.

8. Kefauver Collection. Boone's Creek, Tennessee.

9. Robert Tipton Nave Collection. Elizabethton.

Census Reports

1. Statistical Abstracts of Returns (1820, 1830, 1840, 1850, and 1860).

2. Population Schedules for Carter County (1830, 1840, and 1850), microfilm, Lawson McGhee Library, Knoxville.

State Archives Collections

1. Tax Lists, 1796, 1797, and 1799.

2. County Court Clerks Reports (Varied).

3. Election Certifications

4. Memorials and Petitions

Laws, Journals, and Official Reports

1. Public and Private Acts, 1796-1861

2. Senate Journal, 1797-1822; 1831-1838

3. Edward Scott, comp., Laws of the State of Tennessee. Two Volumes. Knoxville: Heiskell and Brown, 1821.

4. _____, Report of Superintendent of Public Instruction (Nashville: Various official state printers, 1839, 1841, 1847, 1858-1859.

Books

1. Morris, Eastin. The Tennessee Gazetteer. Nashville: W. Hasell Hunt and Co., 1834.

2. Williams, Samuel C. Early Travels in the Tennessee Country. Johnson City: The Watauga Press, 1928.

Newspapers and Periodicals

1. Brownlow's Tennessee Whig, May, 1839; later renamed Elizabethton Whig (1839-1840); this weekly was moved to Jonesboro and renamed Jonesborough Whig (1840-1849); scattered references from the Knoxville Whig (1850-1861).

2. Scattered references from Jonesborough Republican, 1834.

3. Scattered references in Millennial Harbinger, 1831-1844.

Personal Interviews

1. U. S. G. Ellis, Joe Walker, Mr. and Mrs. Lide Hall, Mr. and Mrs. George Mottern, Pierce Julian, Mr. and Mrs. Allen Cates, George W. Ryan, Mr. and Mrs. Bob Patton, Mrs. Martha (Martin) Anderson, Sam Hyder, Fred Hinkle, Mrs. W. M. Vaught, Mr. and Mrs. J. Frank Seiler, Mrs. Bellamy, Jr., Mrs. B. D. Akard, Mrs. L. W. McCown, Isaac Morrell, Judge W. C. O'Brien, Millard Fitzsimmons, Sr., Mrs. John Snodgrass, and Mrs. Jo Taylor (colored). (These interviews proved the more fruitful ones).

SECONDARY SOURCES

Books

1. Abernethy, Thomas P. *From Frontier to Plantation in Tennessee.* Chapel Hill: The University of North Carolina Press, 1932.

2. Asplund, John. *Register.* (Baltimore: John Asplund, 1792)

3. Augsburg, Paul D. *Bob and Alf Taylor Their Lives and Lectures.* Morristown: Morristown Book Company, 1925.

4. Benedict, David. *General History of the Baptist Denomination.* New York: Lewis Colby and Co., 1848.

5. Brownlow, William G. *Sketches of the Rise, Progress, and Decline of Secession.* Philadelphia: George W. Childs, 1862.

6. Carr, Howard E. *Washington College.* Knoxville: S. B. Newman and Co., 1935.

7. Cole, William E., and William H. Combs. *Tennessee A Political Study.* Knoxville: University of Tennessee Press, 1940.

8. Daily, Hiram. *Villany Exposed.* Marion, Virginia: The Harrisonian Office, 1841.

9. Edwards, Lawrence. The Baptists of Tennessee with Particular Attention to the Primitive Baptists of East Tennessee. Knoxville: unpublished Master's Thesis at the University of Tennessee, 1941.

10. Folmsbee, Stanley J. *Sectionalism and Internal Improvements in Tennessee 1796-1845.* Knoxville: The East Tennessee Historical Society, 1939.

11. Foster, A. P. *Counties of Tennessee.* Nashville: The Department of Education, 1923.

12. _____, *History of Tennessee.* Nashville: Goodspeed Publishing Company, 1887.

13. Hall, Alexander W., comp. *The Christian Register.* Lloydsville, Ohio: Alexander W. Hall, 1848.

14. Hamer, Philip H. *Tennessee A History 1673-1932.* New York: The American Historical Society, 1935, I.

15. Henderson, Archibald. The Conquest of the Old Southwest. New York: The Century Company, 1920.

16. Lester, William S. The Transylvania Colony. Spencer, Indiana: Samuel R. Guard and Co., 1935.

17. M'Anally, D. R. Life and Times of Rev. Samuel Patton, D. D. and Annals of the Holston Conference. St. Louis: Methodist Book Depository, 1859.

18. Middlebrooks, John E. A History of the Rise and Fall of Academies in Tennessee. Nashville: an unpublished Master's Thesis at George Peabody College for Teachers, 1923.

19. Price, R. N. Holston Methodism From Its Origin to the Present Time. Nashville: Publishing House of the Methodist Episcopal Church, South, 1908, III.

20. Ramsey, J. G. M. The Annals of Tennessee to the End of the Eighteenth Century. Philadelphia: Lippincott, Grambo and Co., 1953.

21. Roosevelt, Theodore. The Winning of the West. New York: G. P. Putnam's Sons, 1889, I.

22. Scott, Samuel W. and Samuel P. Angel. History of the 13th Regiment Philadelphia: P. W. Zeigler & Co., 1903.

23. Snodgrass, Charles A. Freemasonry in Tennessee. Nashville: Ambrose Printing Company, 1944.

24. Temple, Oliver P. Notable Men of Tennessee. New York: The Cosmopolitan Press, 1912.

25. Tindell, Samuel W. The Baptists of Tennessee. Kingsport: Southern Publishers, Inc., 1930.

26. Ward, Harold E. Academy Education in Tennessee Prior to 1861. Nashville: an unpublished Master's Thesis at George Peabody College for Teachers, 1926.

27. White, Robert H. Tennessee Its Growth and Progress. Nashville: Robert H. White, Publishers, 1936.

28. Wiley, Bell I. The Plain People of the Confederacy. Baton Rouge: Louisiana State University Press, 1943.

29. Wagner, Harry C. History of the Diciples of Christ in Upper East Tennessee. Knoxville: an unpublished Master's thesis at University of Tennessee, 1943.

30. Williams, Samuel C. *Dawn of Tennessee Valley and Tennessee History*. Johnson City: The Watauga Press, 1937.

31. _____, *Tennessee During the Revolutionary War*. Nashville: The Tennessee Historical Commission, 1944.

32. _____, *History of the Lost State of Franklin*. Johnson City: The Watauga Press, 1924.

33. _____, *Brigadier-General Nathaniel Taylor*. Johnson City: The Watauga Press, 1940.

Magazines

1. Abernethy, Thomas P. "Origin of Whig Party in Tennessee," *Mississippi Valley Historical Review*, XII, 504-522 (March, 1926).

2. Cannon, Walter F. "Four Interpretations of the History of the State of Franklin," (to be published in the East Tennessee Historical Society's *Publications*, No. 22, 1950, 1-32 printer's manuscript copy).

3. Goodpasture, A. V. "The Watauga Association," *American Historical Magazine*, III, 103-120 (April, 1898).

4. Hyder, N. E. "Watauga Old Fields," *American Historical Magazine*, VIII, 253-255 (July, 1903).

5. Hesseltine, William B. "Methodism and Reconstruction in East Tennessee," East Tennessee Historical Society's *Publications*, No. 3, 42-61 (January, 1931).

6. Queener, Vernon M. "East Tennessee Sentiment and the Secession Movement, November, 1850-June, 1861," East Tennessee Historical Society's *Publications*, No. 2, 59-83 (1948).

7. Wagner, Harry C. "The Beginnings of the Christian Church in East Tennessee," East Tennessee Historical Society's *Publications*, No. 20, 49-58 (1948).

8. Whitaker, Arthur P. "The Public School System of Tennessee 1834-1860," *Tennessee Historical Magazine*, II, 30 (March, 1916).

9. Williams, Samuel C. "The First Territorial Division Named for Washington," *Tennessee Historical Magazine*, Series II, Vol. II, 153-169 (April, 1932).

APPENDIX

POPULATION OF CARTER COUNTY (1791-1860)

Year	Whites Male	Female	Total	Negroes Slaves	Free Negroes	Total
1791	710	579	1289	113		1402[a]
1800						4813[b]
1810	1959	1969	3928	269		4197[c]
1820[d]	2306	2178	4484	345	6	4835
1830	3064	2886	5950	460	14	6414
1840	2575	2420	4995	352	22	5369
1850	2987	2924	5911	353	32	6296
1860	3377	3351	6728	374	22	7124

[a]1791 figures from population census taken last Saturday in July, 1791 (WPA Project Washington County List of Taxables, Jonesboro Courthouse)

[b]Goodspeed, op. cit., 360.

[c]Brookes Universal Gazetter, 1823.

[d]Census Reports Abstracts, except 1830 which is from the 1830 microfilm schedules.

SOME ORIGINAL GRANTEES TO LAND IN CARTER COUNTY[a]

On Buffalo Creek

Andrew Taylor
George Williams
John Patton
Christopher McInturff
Evan Shelby
Adam Haun
Samuel Henry
Abraham Cooper
Robert English
Edmond Williams
John Tipton

On Roans Creek

Nathaniel Taylor
Nathaniel Foster
Joseph Sams
John Brown
Lewis Wills
Moses Reynolds
William Cunningham
Samuel Williams
John C. Hamilton
John Potter
Ewings Heatherly
Jacob Heatherick
Thomas Payne
William Griffin
Abraham Boyler
George Perkins
Edward Sweetain
Jessee Hoskins
William Baily Smith
Samuel Tate
David Wagner
William Moreland
Rowland Jenkins
Richard White
William Sharpe
William Wilson
Reuben Stringer

On Gap Creek

Landon Carter
Nathan Lewis
Nathaniel Taylor
Simon Bundy
William Sharp
Thomas Talbot
Matthew Talbot
James Edens
Richard Kite

In Watauga Valley

Samuel Tate
John Pevehouse
Landon Carter
Archibald White
Henry Bogart
John Tate
Zachariah Campbell
Andrew Greer
John Asher
Reuben Roberts
George Emmert
Martin Armstrong
John McCoy
Nathaniel Taylor
Godfrey Carriger
John Carter
Joshua Houghton
Edward Smith
Valentine Sevier, Sr.
Patience Cooper
Benjamin Ward
William Ward
Isaac Lincoln
Thomas Carney
Charles Asher
James Taylor
Moses Campbell

On Stoney Creek

Landon Carter
Thomas Miller
James Phillips

Jacob Beeler
Nathaniel Taylor
Samuel Gardland
John King
William Parker
John Sevier, Jr.
Andrew Greer

On Doe River

John Tipton
Daniel Miller
George Peetree
Weightsell Avery
Ebenezer Scrogs
Jacob He(a)drick
Joseph Greer
James Campbell
Jeremiah Campbell
Landon Carter

On Sinking Creek

John Tipton
William Watson
Jessee Bean
Nicholas Hall
Benjamin Holland
Robert Wilson
Charles Robertson
John Bell
Uriah Hunt
Jessee Hunt
David Jobe
John Young
William McNabb
David Greate
Joseph Tipton
Joseph Crouch
Samuel Bogard

[a] From an analysis of land grants from North Carolina as recorded in the offices of the Register of Deeds, Jonesboro and Elizabethton.

OFFICERS OF CARTER COUNTY (1796 - 1861)[a]

Sheriffs

Nathaniel Taylor	1796-1799
Abraham Byler	1799-1805
Archibald Williams	1805-1813
Andrew Taylor	1813-1821
William B. Carter	1821-1823
William Carter	1823-1829
Alexander Smith	1835-1836
Abraham Tupton	1836-1840
Elijah D. Hardin	1840-1842
Edmond Williams	1842-1848
Albert J. Tipton	1848-1854
Elijah Simerly	1854-1860
John K. Miller	1860-1863

Register of Deeds

Godfrey Carriger, Jr.	1796-1827
Benjamin Brewer	1827-1836
Solomon Hendrix	1836-1840
Malcolm N. Folsom	1840-1844
Isaac H. Brown	1840-1850
W. Williams	1850-1851
Jackson G. Fellers	1851-1860
Joseph Taylor	1860-1870

Trustees

John MacLin	1796-?
William Peoples, Jr.	1811-1813
David McNabb	1813-1817
Willie W. Williams	1817-1819
Ezekial Smith	1825-1836
Joseph O'Brien	1836-1840
Samuel Drake	1840-1844
George Emmert	1844-1846
John W. Hyder	1846-1852
Issac H. Brown	1852-1856
John T. Carriger	1856-1862

[a]Goodspeed, op. cit., 911-913; the writer has seen most of these officers listed as such many times during his research.

Circuit Court Clerks

Alfred M. Carter	1810-1836
George C. Williams	1836-1840
Carrick W. Nelson	1840-1846
Isaac P. Tipton	1846-1854
John Singletary	1854-1861
James A. Burrow	1861-1862

County Court Clerks

George Williams	1796-1836
Malcolm N. Folsom	1836-1840
James L. Bradley	1840-1878

CHAIRMEN OF THE COUNTY COURT (1836-1860)[a]

1836	Johnson Hampton, Sr.
1837	George Emmert
1838	George Emmert
1839	Isaac Tipton
1840	Isaac Tipton
1841	Isaac Tipton
1842	David Nelson
1843	Malcolm N. Folsom
1844	Thomas Gourley
1845	Thomas Gourley
1846	Isaac Tipton
1847	George Emmert
1848	Thomas Gourley
1849	Malcolm N. Folsom
1850	George W. Peoples
1851	Robert J. Allen
1852	**Thomas Gourley**
1853	Henry Little
1854	Thomas Gourley
	James H. Martin
1855	James W. Renfro
1856	Henderson Roberts
1857	C. W. Nelson, county judge presiding
1858	James H. Martin
1859	R. C. White
1860	R. C. White

[a] County Court Minutes, years indicated.

LIST OF THE EARLY MAGISTRATES IN CARTER COUNTY SHOWING DATE OF APPOINTMENT, ETC.

1790

(Appointed by William Blount, Governor of the Southwest Territory)

Landon Carter Andrew Greer Joshua Kelly
Charles Robertson Edmond Williams

1801

Alexander Doran Christian Stover John Carter
Joseph Thompkins Roland Jenkins Thomas Maxwell

1803

Hugh White

1805

Abraham Henry Nathan Hendricks Joseph Sands
Joseph Mason Benjamin C. Harris William Guat (Gott)

1806

(Resigned) Andrew Taylor Andrew Greer
John Wright

1809

John Scoggins Benjamin C. Harris Henry Hammons
James Johnston John L. Williams Lawson White
James Keyes Johnson Hampton John Bogard

1811

(Resigned)
Matthias Wagner Godfrey Carriger Alfred M. Carter
Christian Carriger Benjamin C. Harris Nathan Hendrix
Joshua Royston John Nave Isaac Campbell
William B. Carter

1812

Samuel Tipton

LIST OF THE EARLY MAGISTRATES IN CARTER COUNTY
SHOWING DATE OF APPOINTMENT, ETC. (Continued)

1815

William Carter   James Keys

1817

Joseph Renfro   Thomas Johnson   William Tompkins
Caleb Smith   Samuel Tipton   Daniel Wagner
Daniel Stover   William Graham   Nicholas Smith
Jesse Cole

1819

William B. Carter   Hugh Jenkins   John Wright
Thomas Evans   Isaac Campbell

186

LOCATION OF FIRST CIVIL DISTRICTS AND NAMES OF FIRST MAGISTRATES ELECTED BY PEOPLE (1836)[a]

District and Location	Names of the Justices of the Peace
#1 - Fish Springs	William Lewis and Johnson Hampton, Jr.
#2 - Crab Orchard (present Roan Mountain)	John J. Wilson, Elisha Smith
#3 - Tiger and Simerly Creek Dove River Cove (Hampton)	Meremiah Campbell, Johnson Hampton, Sr.
#4 - Buffalo Creek and Greasy Cover (Unicoi)	Edmond Williams, William Peoples
#5 - Gap Creek and Powder Branch	Jonathan Hyder, John L. Williams
#6 - Sinking Creek Cedar Grove	Thomas Gourley, William Williams
#7 - Elizabethton (old town) Valley Forge and part of new town	Aquilla Moore (later Isaac Tipton)
#8 - Turkeytown, Range and Keenburg	George Emmert, Joel Cooper
#9 - Watauga Valley, Hunter, Siam, Blue Springs	William Allen, Henry C. Nave
#10- Upper Stoney Creek	Jonathan Lipps, John T. Bowers

KNOWN DISTRICT POLLING PLACES AFTER 1836[b]

First District	House of Lawson Goodwin on Watauga River
Second District	House of Elijah Smith
Third District	Old John Simerly place near Johnston Hampton
Fourth District	Isaac Williams Store
Fifth District	House of Archibald Williams
Sixth District	James Hickey on Watauga River
Seventh District	Elizabethton (Courthouse)
Eighth District	House of John Hendrix
Ninth District	Christian Carriger Mill
Tenth District	House of David Forbes on Stoney Creek

---

[a] From copy of commission on file in office of the County Court Clerk, Elizabethton.

[b] Above information contained in description of the civil districts and the plat of the county sent to Secretary of State, Nashville, after the county was districted in accordance with 1836 law. The document is dated February 10, 1836, and is attested by John L. Lusk, J. P. and is signed by the county districting committee composed of Taylor McNabb, Christian Carriger, Jeremiah Campbell, and George Emmert. Tenn. Archives.

MEMBERS OF THE COUNTY COURT

1842-48

1st District	–	William Lewis and Smith Campbell
2nd District	–	John J. Wilson and Solomon B. Snyder*
3rd District	–	Johnson Hampton and John W. Hyder
4th District	–	George W. Peoples and William W. Smith
5th District	–	Lorenzo D. Rowe and John L. Williams
6th District	–	Thomas Gourley and Joel Cooper
7th District	–	Isaac P. Tipton, M. N. Folsom, and Henderson Roberts
8th District	–	George Emmert and Henry Little
9th District	–	John Carriger and Elijah D. Harden
10th District	–	Benjamin Cole and James Berry

(*Snyder was replaced by Elisha Smith May, 1844.)

1848-1854

1st District	–	Johnson Hampton, Jr. and Richard C. White
2nd District	–	John J. Wilson and Ansel Carden
3rd District	–	Johnson Hampton, Sr. and Jacob Simerly
4th District	–	William W. Smith and George W. Peoples
5th District	–	James H. Martin and A. S. Y. Lusk
6th District	–	Thomas Gourley and J. H. Hyder
7th District	–	Isaac P. Tipton and Malcolm N. Folsom, William C. O'Brien
8th District	–	Henry Little and James W. Renfro
9th District	–	John Carriger and Robert J. Allen
10th District	–	John N. Harden and Pleasant Williams

1854-1860

1st District	–	Ansel Carden and John P. Cable*
2nd District	–	John J. Wilson and Nicholas Smith
3rd District	–	William Snyder and Benjamin Dyer*
4th District	–	George W. Peoples and John Daniel
5th District	–	James H. Martin and Edmond Williams
6th District	–	Jonathan H. Hyder and John Snodgrass
7th District	–	M. N. Folsom, Henderson Roberts,* Lawson W. Fletcher
8th District	–	James W. Renfro and James Hickey
9th District	–	Robert J. Allen and Jackson D. Carriger
10th District	–	Thomas Heatherly and Andrew R. Ritchie
11th District	–	Joel S. O'Brien and William Woodby

(* Cable was replaced by Richard C. White
 * Dyer was replaced by Lawson W. Hampton
 * Roberts was replaced by Gilson O. Collins)

(Information concerning courts for 1842-48 and 1848-54 obtained from a study of the County Court Minutes. Tenn. Archives, Nashville, election returns, source for 1854-60 court information.)

PASTORS OF THE SINKING CREEK BAPTIST CHURCH[a]

1. Matthew Talbott   (Tradition: before 1783)
2. Joshua Kelly   1783-1791
3. James Chambers   1791-1793 <u>circum</u>
4. Jonathan Mulkey   1794-1821 (about 27 years)
5. Reese Bayless   1821-1852 (about 31 years)
6. William C. Newell   1852-1858
7. James B. Stone   1858-1860
8. E. Spurgin   1860-1861
9. J. H. Hyder   1861-1870

CLERKS OF THE SINKING CREEK BAPTIST CHURCH[a]

1. David Jobe   during the 1780's
2. David Greate   during the 1790's
3. Daniel Stover   1803-1828
4. Peter Kuhn   1828-1831
5. Thomas D. Love   1831-1833
6. William Pugh   1833-1835
7. Richard Carr   1835-1839
8. William Pugh   1839-1843
9. William White   1843-1846
10. William Hatcher   3 months
11. Robert H. Mulkey   1846-1848
12. Alfred Carr   1848-1868

CHARTER MEMBERS OF THE STONEY CREEK BAPTIST CHURCH[a]

1. Henry Nave and wife   13. Elizabeth Nave
2. Polly Ivy   14. Anna Buckels
3. Joseph Cable   15. Rebekah Nave
4. Elesander Moten   16. Nancy Berry
5. Elender Evens   17. Levicy Carriger
6. Valentine Bowers   18. Jacob Cole
7. Geney Moten   19. Scily Cole
8. James Peters   20. Elizabeth Hathaway
9. Abigal Bowers   21. Samuel Musgrave
10. Lydia Taylor   22. Clerissa Evens
11. Thomas Evens   23. Jariah Gentry
12. Sarah Musgraves   24. Rebekah Cable

[a]The minutes of the Sinking Creek Baptist Church

PASTORS OF THE STONEY CREEK BAPTIST CHURCH[a]

1. Reese Bayless — 1822
2. Leonard Bowers — 1823-1826
3. Benjamin White — 1827-1840
4. Jonathan Lipps — 1841-1845
5. Valentine Bowers — 1846-1849
   (also served 1853, 1859-1860)
6. William C. Newell — 1852, 1854
7. J. B. Stone — 1856
8. J. B. Vann — 1857
9. J. H. Hyder — 1861

(R. N. Campbell was a reported member, a licensed preacher, and probably assisted.)

CHARTER MEMBERS OF THE ELIZABETHTON BAPTIST CHURCH

1. Rebecca Humphreys
2. Samuel B. Peterson/Patterson/
3. Selina Tipton
4. Elizabeth Lyon
5. Christian C. Lovelace
6. Elijah Lacy
7. Charity Blevin/s/
8. Susanna Tipton

<u>From Sinking Creek</u>
9. Mason R. Lyon
10. Leonard Hart
11. Phoebe Hart

<u>From Laurel Fork</u>
12. Martha Tipton
13. Sarah Miller
14. Abraham Tipton
15. Thomas C. Johnson
16. Nancy J. Johnson

<u>From Watauga</u>
17. Sarah Huffman
18. Deliah Adams
19. Alfred C. Lovelace
20. Susannah Humphreys
21. Mary Lovelace
22. Henry Adams
23. Isaac Lovelace
24. Alfred Lovelace
25. Joseph Renfro
26. Jonathan Crouch
27. Elijah D. Harden
28. Levicy Harden
29. Elizabeth Williams
30. Levicy Gifford
31. Edy Carter (colored)

[a] Compiled from the Minutes, Sinking Creek Baptist Church.

[b] Compiled from the Minutes, Elizabethton Baptist Church.

EARLY METHODIST CIRCUIT RIDERS[a]

Circuit Headquarters at Elizabethton

1833	D. T. Fulton
1834	B. McC. Roberts
1835	William G. Brownlow
1836	J. R. Sensebaugh
1837	William H. Rogers
1838	G. W. Alexander
1839	T. K. Harmon
1840	W. L. Turner
1841	("to be supplied")
1842	Daniel Payne
1843	A. N. Harris
1844	Edward W. Chanceaulme
1845	George K. Snapp
1846	Silas H. Cooper
1847	William Milburn
1848	William Milburn
1849	William T. Dorrell
1850	Ambrose G. Worley
1851	John M. McTeer
1852	Willis Ingle
1853	Willis Ingle
1854	H. West
1855	James T. Smith
1856	Andrew G. Copeland
1857	John R. Stradley
1858	"to be supplied"
1859	James Mahoney
1860	Gaston M. Massey
1861	Willis Ingle

Circuit Headquarters at Watauga

1853	William W. Smith
1854	William W. Smith
1855	Andrew Copeland
1856	T. M. Dula
1857	William H. Cooper
1858	George Creamer
1859	"to be supplied"
1860	"to be supplied"
1861	W. P. Cooper

[a] Compiled from the Minutes of the Annual Conferences of the Methodist Episcopal Church and Minutes of the Annual Conferences of the Methodist Episcopal Church South.

CHARTER MEMBERS OF THE FIRST PRESBYTERIAN CHURCH OF ELIZABETHTON[a]

1. Alfred M. Carter
2. William D. Jones
3. Benjamin Brewer
4. Ann S. Jones
5. Mary C. Taylor
6. Mary Taylor
7. Elizabeth Smith
8. Mary Ann Tipton
9. Ruth McLeod
10. William Mitchell
11. Elizabeth Blair
12. Margaret Blair
13. Evalina B. Carter
14. Ann S. McLin
15. Sarah S. Brewer
16. Isaac Taylor
17. Jane Taylor

MEMBERS SOON AFTERWARDS ADDED

1. Elizabeth C. Taylor
2. Evalina E. C. Taylor
3. Nathaniel G. Taylor
4. Martha Renfro
5. Orrey Humphreys
6. Moses Huffman
7. William Huffman
8. Thomas B. Huffman
9. Margaret Huffman
10. Finetty Huffman
11. Ann E. Huffman
12. James C. Simpson
13. Mary Simpson
14. Martha Powell
15. Jacob Cameron
16. Jane Cameron
17. Jane S. Gott
18. Elizabeth Nicholas
19. David W. Carter
20. S. D. Carter
21. Sam'l P. Carter
22. William B. Carter, Jr.
23. Elizabeth L. Drake
24. Eliza Drake
25. Mary Drake
26. Mary Ann Smith
27. Sarah M. Stover
28. George A. Duffield
29. Mrs. Abraham Drake

EARLY MINISTERS OF THE CHURCH

Name of the Minister	When Served	How Often
1. James McLin	"for some time after its organization"	"half his time"
2. James G. Ward	"until about the year 1834"	/probably half time/
3. J. W. Cunningham	1834-1841	"half his time"
4. William A. Taylor		
5. James McLin	/1841-1844/	
6. Albert G. Taylor	Nov. 1846-Jan. 1848	
7. Ira Morey	April-August 1849	"once in three weeks"
8. Alexander A. Doak (Old School)	Dec. 1850-Dec. 1851	"once a month"
9. A. H. Sloat	"for a few months"	
10. J. M. Hoffmeister	May 30, 1859-1861	half time

[a] Compiled from the Minutes of the First Presbyterian Church.

EARLY MEMBERS OF THE BUFFALO CREEK CHRISTIAN CHURCH

Isaac Taylor	Hensen Hunt
Susana Curtis	John Curtis
Ira Howard	Rebeckah Williams
Michael Hyder	Nancy Young
Nancy Young	James Gourley
James I. Tipton	Hiter Hunt
James I. Tipton's colored woman	
	Jonathan Kelly
Elizabeth Ellis	Michael Hyder, Sen.
Adam Loudermilk	Jabez Murry
Adam McInturff	John Wright
Solomen Hendrix	John Howard
Samuel Wright	John Orton
Dinah Peoples, colored	Betsy Taylor, the doctor's wife
John McKeehen	
Thomas, colored woman	Betsy Ellis
Betsy and Alfred Blevins	Pinkney Williams

[a]Compiled from Michael E. Hyder church treasury report in the Professor Sam Hyder Collection, Milligan College, Tennessee.

BIOGRAPHICAL SKETCH OF GEORGE DUFFIELD[a]

George Duffield, Carter County's first educator of any importance, was born about 1778 and was the son of the Rev. Samuel Duffield. Young Duffield came to Tennessee about 1799 or 1800 and settled at Greeneville where he began the practice of law. While at Greeneville, being probably the best educated young man there, he became interested in the small struggling Greeneville College. He became a close friend to the president of the institution and particularly concerned himself with the small college library. It is believed that he was instrumental in securing quite a number of valuable books and financial assistance from Presbyterian friends back in Philadelphia.

The earliest reference that identifies him with Carter County is to be found in a deed that he witnessed on February 12, 1800, to a land transaction between Andrew Greer, Sr., and Andrew Greer, Jr. Sometime near the end of 1806, he married Sallie Stewart Carter (March 6, 1789--April 5, 1879), daughter of Landon and Elizabeth MacLin Carter. In selecting Duffield Miss Carter turned down John Rhea, the first district congressman, who apparently could not "compete with the gallant and cultured Duffield." After marriage he removed to Elizabethton to practice law and probably took a leading part in the management of the estates and affairs of his deceased father-in-law. His legal services would have been much in demand since the Carter interests were great and varied.

Duffield gained prominence as a lawyer and was offered the facated seat of Judge Hugh L. White in 1814 when the latter resigned from the Tennessee Supreme Court. Probably because of his duties in connection with the management of the Carter estate and because he seemed not to have aspired to political office, he declined the governor's offer. The very tender of such a high legal position indicates that Duffield was a legalist of some note by this time.

While at Greeneville George Duffield met another young lawyer who later achieved national prominence. This acquaintanceship led Andrew Jackson in 1803 to appoint him as an aide-de-camp. He held a similar position as well as adjutant to General Nathaniel Taylor in 1814 against the Indians and the British at Mobile. He must have been a favorite of General Taylor's. One of their camps is what is now Alabama was known as Camp Duffield. Later during the campaign against the Creeks General Taylor picked up a small Creek Indian lad and brought him back to Carter County. He named the young fellow

---

[a]From extensive research into deeds, Elizabeth Carter's will, census reports, academy papers, laws of Tennessee, personal interviews, genealogical records. Especially helpful was Judge Samuel C. Williams' lecture and typewritten notes which he used for a lecture at Tusculum College about 1941. Williams referred to Duffield as "Friend of the Library.")

George Duffield "after a celebrated young lawyer . . . . living in Elizabethton". (Later this Indian married a Negro and became the ancestor of the colored Duffield family in Elizabethton.)

Undoubtedly George Duffield took an active interest in the academy in Elizabethton which was named in his honor. Since he was named first on the board of trustees appointed in 1806, it can safely be assumed that he was the chairman of the group. (According to tradition of the Duffields now living in Carter and Johnson counties, the first academy building was constructed about 1809. These Duffields are direct descendants of the George Duffield for whom the school was named.) In the original plan of the city of Elizabethton, lot #15 was set aside by the county commissioners and reserved for the building of a church. A petition to the general assembly about 1820 confirms the fact that the academy building was used for church purposes. (It is doubted by the writer that Duffield gave the site where the school was constructed despite a tradition to that effect.)

George Duffield lived to see the small school through the first fifteen years of its existence. He died June 28, 1823, survived by his widow and three children, Elizabeth Carter Duffield who married Alfred W. Taylor, George A. Duffield, a doctor who died in 1844, and Samuel Landon Duffield whose descendants still live in the region. About three years later Mrs. Duffield married William Brewer of Elizabethton. Both the Duffields and the Brewers were active members of the Presbyterian Church. Research has so far been unfruitable in trying to locate the grave of the first George Duffield.

It is a fitting memorial to the memory of George Duffield, Carter's first educator, a lawyer of prominence, military and business man, that even to this day the school which he largely helped to found still bears his name.

OFFICERS, TEACHERS, AND STUDENTS AT DUFFIELD ACADEMY [a]

Chairman		Secretary and Treasurer	
1840	Hiram Daily	1840	Alfred W. Taylor
1845	Alfred W. Carter	1842-48	Jacob Cameron
1848-52	John Singletary	1850-57	Isaac P. Tipton
1858-59	Jonas H. Keen	1857-61	John Singletary
1859	A. Hart		(upon his death January 14, 1861, Abraham Jobe succeeded him.)

Date	Name of Teacher	Remarks	Pay
1840-41	Wood Furman	(probably taught 3 sessions—15 months)	
1841 Nov.	Rev. James McLin	(Goodspeed's account says 2 years)	$240.00
May 1845	Rev. Stephen Fisk		$106.12½
1848-1850	W. Matthew and Burket	5 sessions of 5 months each	$500.00
1850-1	Alfred H. Matthews	1850 census lists him as "Professor in Academy"	
1853-1855	L. W. Hover and Wife	7 sessions and a part of another	$825.00
1855-1856	W. C. Bowman Elizabeth C. Singletary	1 session - 5 months	76.00
1857-1858	J. L. Shannon	2 sessions	$500.00
1859	L. L. Tipton	1 session	111.00
1859-1860	John A. Tipton, lawyer	1 session	114.31
1860-1861	James I. R. Boyd	Goodspeed's account	
1861	Thomas W. Newman		214.30

Student	Tuition	Year 1858	Student	Tuition
Lawson Hyder	$ 7.50		Andrew Hyder	$5.00
Bayless Miller	7.50		Marshall Woods	7.50
Robert Nelson	10.00		Robert Holly	7.50
William Rhea	7.50		Alfred Carter	7.50
John Tipton	5.00		Milton Devault	5.00
Amanda J. Hyder	5.00		John Dodgen	5.00
Elbert Jordan	5.00		Joel Mast	5.00
David Carter	5.00		Josephine Nelson	7.50
Eva Tipton	7.50		Hildy Nelson	7.50
Sallie Nelson	5.00		Ada Newell	5.00
Cordelia Newell	5.00		Ferd Singletary	10.00
Hiram Dodgen	5.00		Caleb Emmert	7.50
Windfield Tipton	5.00		Lydia Barker	5.00

OFFICERS, TEACHERS, AND STUDENTS AT DUFFIELD ACADEMY (Continued)[a]

Students	Tuition	Students	Tuition
William Smith	5.00	Margaret Barker	7.50
Susan Smith	5.00	Mollie Taylor	7.50
Ann Johnson	7.50	Mary Johnson	7.50
Cordelia Hyder Creed	7.50	Landon Lusk	7.50

[a] 1848 Academy Papers, scattered notices in Elizabethton Whig, 1839-40, and Jonesborough Whig, 1840-1846.

DISTRICT COMMON SCHOOL COMMISSIONERS ELECTED BY THE PEOPLE 1838[a]

First District

Ezekiel Smith, Jr.
William Lewis
John Berry
Jeremiah Whaley
Danville W. White

Second District

Elijah Smith
John W. Lacy
Solomon B. Snyder
John D. Sheffield
Obediah Leonard

Third District

Johnson Hampton, Sr.
Johnson Hampton, Jr.
James F. Cass
John W. Hyder
William Snyder

Fifth District

William Greer
Ephraim Buck
J. H. Hyder
Samuel W. Williams
Edmond Williams

Sixth District

Isaac P. Tipton
James Clark
John Boyd
Joel Cooper
Thomas P. Ensor

Seventh District

Abraham Tipton
William G. Brownlow
John Hathaway
Thomas Badgett
Robert Reeve

Eighth District

Samuel Drake
John Alexander
Jacob Range
Lucas Emmert
Solomon Hendrix

Ninth District

Christian Carriger
Godfrey Nave
John T. Bowers
Henry C. Nave
Daniel Stover

Tenth District

William Allen
Jonathan Lipps
Elliot Carriger
Benjamin Cole
Alfred Cole

Fourth District

John Wright
Thomas McInturff
Jacob Akard

---

[a] County Court Minutes, June, 1838, pp. 92-94.

[b] Ibid., June, 1842, p. 114.

COMPARISON OF SCHOLASTIC POPULATION (COMMON SCHOOLS)[a]

District	1839	1842	1844	1850
1	88	80	100	51
2	59	59	130	78
3	85	65	82	80
4	121	160	271	69
5	213	194	252	211
6	123	123	203	88
7	206	159	255	63 and 115
8	152	142	239	127
9	140	--	190	111
10	170	203	250	161

[a] 1839 figures from Report of Superintendent of Public Instruction
1842 Minutes of the County Court, August, 1842, 121
1844 Minutes of the County Court, August, 1844, 257
1850 Census "Number attended school within the year"
Thus it appears that about 60 to 70 per cent of school-age children had attended school during the year 1850.

COMMON SCHOOLS, THEIR LOCATION AND PATRONS[a]

Name of School and Location	Families Whose Children Probably Attended
1. School "in the Neck" (present Siam Valley, land given by Daniel Stover)	Matthias VanHuss, David Dugger, John L. Bowers, Leonard Bowers, Jr., Jones Allen, Joel D. Nave, Wiley Ellis, Daniel Stover
2. "Nave School" later called "Davis School" (Near where Judge Ben Allen now lives)	Henry C. Nave, Robert C. Crow, David Bowers, Sr., Daniel S. Bowers, I. H. Brown
3. "Old Fisher Field School" (near mouth of Brown's Branch, above Hampton on road to Tiger Valley)	Michael Grindstaff, John Hyder, Elijah Simerly, William Fondern, Nicodemus Johnson, George Morton, John Hill
4. "Anderson School" (Head of Buffalo Creek, now called Cave Springs)	Isaac H. Anderson, George Swaner, N. G. Taylor, Jackson Peoples, William Keen, Isaac Buck, David Haynes, George Bowman
5. "Oak Grove School" sometimes called "Hyder School," (up Powder Branch, on land given by Sam Hyder)	Jessee Hyder, Billy Hyder, Michael E. Hyder, Sammy McKen, Ben Walker
6. "Carriger School," later called "Watauga Academy," (not to be confused with a still later Watauga Academy near Butler) (stood on lands given by Godfrey Carriger, Jr., opposite Nave's mill.	Godfrey Carriger, Christian Carriger, Caleb B. Cox, Henry Nave, John Taylor, Mordecai Williams, David Nave, William Bishop, Israel Cole, Christian C. Nave, John T. Allen, John Nave, Jr., Benjamin White, Jeremiah Cannon
7. "Bell School," sometimes called "O'Brien School" or "Davis School," (at Limestone Cove, near Grindstaff cemetery)	David Bell, Nathan Birchfield, William Baker, Ezekiel Grindstaff, Thomas Gouge, William and Eppy Wood, Uriah Banks
8. "Jones Chapel School" (Solomon Jones' place at Unicoi)	Solomon Jones, Bill Blevins, Benjamin Swingle, Leonard Swingle, Ken McLaughan, Pete Berry

[a] Personal interview with residents in various communities. These proved especially helpful: Pierce Julian, "Uncle" Ike Morrell, Ben Walker, Lide Hall, Mrs. Allen Cates, Mrs. Martha Anderson.

9. "Buffalo Creek School," (present site of Milligan College) — George "Dot" Williams, Samuel Williams, Jim Anderson, George Williams, Sam Williams, Pickney Williams, Wiley Boren, George Ensor, George Haun, James Gourley, Joseph Price, Sam W. Hyder, John Quincy Williams.

10. "Taylor School," (near Okolona on Erwin Highway) — Isaac Taylor, Sam Simerly.

11. "Heaton Creek School," (Heaton Creek Community, beyond Roan Mountain) — James N. Julian, Washington Heaton, Johnson Hampton, Frank Miller, Daniel Shell.

12. "Crab Orchard School," (Crab Orchard Community) — Elijah Smith, Alfred Johnson, _____ Miller.

13. "Rain Hill School," (near top of Whitehead Hill) — Jim Whitehead, William Snyder, _____ Chambers.

14. "Shell Creek School," (Shell Creek Community, near present Cloudland) — Hamilton H. Ray, William D. Wilson, Baker Snyder, Finley Shell, John Shell, Jacob Perkins.

15. "Hughes School" — David Hughes, David Kitzmiller, Alfred Carr, Pughs, Hatchers, Kuhns

16. "Range School," sometimes called "Moody School" — George Lottern, David Holly, Radford Ellis, Jim Range, Slagles

NEGROES, SLAVE AND FREE, IN CARTER COUNTY[a]

Year	Free Colored Male	Female	Total	Slave Male	Female	Total	TOTAL
1800							185
1810						269	269
1820	2	4	6	177	168	345	351
1830	6	8	14	226	234	460	474
1840	14	8	22	179	173	352	374
1850	12	20	32	167	186	353	385
1860	10	12	22	181	193	374	386

[a] The 1800 figure is estimated on the basis of the 1830, 1860, and 1797 tax list as compared with known totals of the 1830, and 1860 census findings. The 1810 figure is taken from William Darby, Brookes Universal Gazetter (Philadelphia: Bennett and Walton, 1823) 167. All other figures taken from census abstracts for years indicated.

TABLE OF DISTRIBUTION OF SLAVES (1830, 1840, and 1860)[a]

Number of Slaveowners	1830	1840	1860
Having 1 slave	47	20	29
Having 2 slaves	13	13	13
Having 3 slaves	8	11	9
Having 4 slaves	6	11	3
Having 5 slaves	9	1	7
Having 6 slaves	5	1	1
Having 7 slaves	2	4	2
Having 8 slaves	7	1	3
Having 9 slaves	2	3	5
Having 10 and under 15	6	6	6
Having 15 and under 20	3	1	1
Having 20 and under 30	1	3	2
Having 30 and under 40	1	0	1

By name the largest slaveholders were:[b]

1830
1. Mary Lincoln   37
2. Jonathan Hickey   21
3. Mary Taylor   19
4. David Wagner, Sr.   18
5. James F. Taylor   17

1840
1. William Stover   23
2. William B. Carter   21
3. James Hickey   21
4. Mary C. Taylor   18
5. John Kuhn   14

1860
1. Robert Love   13
2. A. W. Taylor, heirs 13
3. William G. Baker   11
4. J. J. Hyder, Sr.   7
5. William Stover   7

[a]Compiled from the Population Schedules and Abstracts of the Census Reports for 1830 and 1840. The 1860 figures represent only the taxable Negroes represented on the 1860 Carter Tax List in Office of County Court Clerk.

[b]Ibid.

SLAVEOWNERS, SHOWING CIVIL DISTRICT, NUMBER OF SLAVES OWNED[a]

District #1
- Mary White — 3
- Johnson Potter — 1

District #2
- Elijah Smith — 1
- Johnson Hampton — 7
- Hamilton Hampton — 6

District #3
- Jeremiah Campbell — 3
- John R. Carriger — 1
- Alexander Lacy — 3
- James Ervin — 1
- Samuel B. Patterson — 1

District #4
- Edmond Williams — 1
- Isaac Anderson — 2
- William Peoples — 1

District #5
- Nathaniel McNabb — 1
- David Pugh — 10
- John L. Roe — 2
- Harrison Hunt — 2
- John L. Williams — 10
- George D. Williams — 5
- George Williams — 3
- Pinckney P. Williams — 1
- Alfred W. Taylor — 10
- Caswell C. Taylor — 4

District #6
- James Boyd, Sr. — 9
- John Kuhn — 14
- Susannah Hughes — 2
- Marchey Hilton — 1
- Leonard Morgan — 1
- Mary Humphreys — 9
- Thomas P. Ensor — 1
- Mary C. Taylor — 18
- James Hickey — 21
- Jonathan Taylor — 1
- Joseph Hyder — 1

District #7
- William B. Carter — 21
- Jacob Cameron — 2
- Abraham Tipton — 1
- Leonard M. Swingle — 1
- William Rockhold — 3
- William Rhea — 4
- Abner McLeod — 1
- Hiram Daily — 2
- David Nelson — 7
- John Jobe — 9
- Benjamin Brewer — 11
- David W. Carter — 1
- Joseph Powell — 3
- James O'Brien — 2
- Matthias Keen — 7
- Elijah Hathaway — 4
- Susannah Deloach — 3
- Wood Furman — 3
- James P. Housley — 3
- James J. Angel — 11
- Joseph Underwood — 4
- Landon D. Carter — 4

District #8
- Jonathan Range — 4
- Archibald Vest — 3
- Alexander P. Woods — 1
- William Carter — 4
- James Turner — 2
- Samuel Drake — 4

District #9
- John Carriger — 4
- Robert C. Crowe — 4
- David Nave — 1
- Mary Madison — 1
- John Hickie — 2
- Christian Carriger — 8
- Isaac L. Carriger — 2
- George M. Carriger — 2
- William Stover — 23
- Daniel Stover — 4

District #10
- David Taylor — 7
- David Bishop — 2
- Peter Fraisure — 2

[a]As abstracted from the Sixth Census (1840), Population Schedules, Tennessee (microfilm).

SLAVEOWNERS ACCORDING TO DISTRICTS, NUMBER, AND VALUE OF SLAVES (1860 and 1861)[a]

District & Name	1860 Number	1860 Value	1861 Number	1861 Value
First	(2	1500)	(4	2300)
John Smith	1	$1000	1	$800
John H. Smith	1	500	1	300
Edd T. Smith			2	1200
Second	(5	4400)	(5	4000)
Sarah Hampton	1	1000	1	800
Wright Moreland	3	2500	3	2600
H. H. Ray	1	900	1	600
Third	(7	7200)	(9	6200)
Alexander J. Campbell	1	900	2	1200
T. Nat Campbell, heirs	1	900	1	600
Lawson W. Hampton, Jr.	3	3000	3	2000
Sarah Lacy	2	2400	2	1600
Elijah Simerly	-	-	1	800
Fourth	(9	6400)	(9	5000)
William J. Peoples	1	800	1	600
Elizabeth Peoples			1	600
William Peeples	1	800		
N. G. Taylor	6	3800	6	3000
John Wright	1	1000	1	800
Fifth	(18	18,200)	(17	10,500)
James Hughes, heirs	3	2900	3	1800
Moses A. Miller	2	1900	1	600
Catherine Pugh	1	900	1	600
Samuel L. Rowe	1	600	1	600
Rachel Rowe	1	900	-	-
John L. Rowe, heirs	-	-	1	600
Caswell C. Taylor	4	3600	4	2400
S. W. & Geo. D. Williams	3	2900	3	3000
Pheneas Williams	2	1900	1	500
Edmond Williams	1	800	1	600
S. W. Williams, Jr.	-	-	1	800

[a] Abstracted from the County Tax Lists for 1860 and 1861 (County Court Clerk's Office, Elizabethton).

SLAVEOWNERS ACCORDING TO DISTRICTS, NUMBER, AND VALUE OF SLAVES (1860 and 1861) Continued

District & Name	Number 1860	Value 1860	Number 1861	Value 1861
Sixth	(49	39,600)	(48	29,100)
William P. Brewer	3	2500	3	1800
Noah Daniel, heirs	2	1600	2	1600
J. H. Hyder, Sr.	7	6000	6	5000
Robert Love	15	11700	15	11700
Hanah Love, heirs	2	1200	–	0
_____ Loudermilk	2	1200	–	–
A. M. C. Taylor	3	1800	3	1500
A. W. Taylor, heirs	13	10400	13	8000
Isaac P. Tipton	4	3200	5	4000
Charles Thompson	–	–	1	600
Seventh	(15	12000)	(20	11,700)
David W. Carter	2	1800	3	1800
James T. Carter, heirs	2	1500	3	1300
A. M. Carter, heirs	5	4000	7	3500
Jacob Cameron, heirs	2	1500	1	1600
William R. Fitzsimmons	2	1500	1	1200
William W. Hockhold	1	900	1	800
Albert J. Tipton	1	800	1	600
C. W. Folsom	–	–	1	600
James T. Gillespie	–	–	1	1000
Abraham Jobe	–	–	1	300
Eighth	(5	3200)	(6	4800)
Eleana D. Range	1	600	1	600
Nathaniel L. Taylor	1	800	1	1000
Archabold Vest	2	1800	2	1600
Emily Cox, widow	–	–	1	800
G. T. Magee	–	–	1	800
Ninth	(29	23,700)	(38	21,375)
J. H. Bowers	1	800	–	–
Margaret Carriger	1	800	1	800
Robert C. Crow	2	1800	3	2200
Daniel Stover, heirs	3	2500	3	2200
David L. Stover, heirs	3	2500	3	2300
S. M. Stover	7-	5600	9	6500
William Stover	7	5600	5	3200
Daniel Stover	3	2500	5	2600
William S. Thomas	2	1600	2	1400
I. H. Brown	–	–	1	800
Margret Job	–	–	1	700
Noah Mast	–	–	3	1675
Fedsick Thomas	–	–	2	1400

SLAVEOWNERS ACCORDING TO DISTRICTS, NUMBER OF SLAVES
AND VALUE OF SLAVES (1860 and 1861) Continued

	1860		1861	
District & Name	Number	Value	Number	Value
Tenth	(2	1800)	(3	1800)
Rueben Brooks	2	1800	3	1800
Eleventh	(17	13,600)	(19	11,900)
William Baker	4	3600	3	2000
William G. Baker	11	8800	11	7200
David Baker	2	1200	2	1000
F. H. Hammon	-	-	3	1700

TOTALS: 1860   158 $131,600.00
         1861   178   108,675.00

INDEX

(Note: This does not include an index of the appendix.)

Adams, Alan A. 136
    David, 104
    James, 134
Allen, John T., 146n
    William, 146n
Angel, James J., 109, 132
    S. P., 167n
    Samuel, 167n
Andersonx, Isaac, 157
Arrants, Louise, 122

Badgett, Thomas, 109n
Bakers 159n
Barton, Isaac, 75n
Bass, Jeremish, 149, 150, 151
Bayless, John, 97, John, Jr., 99n
Bayless, Reese, 80, 81, 83, 85n 88, 94
Bean, William, 14n
Bedley, Sarah, 80
Bell, John, 67, 70
    Rev. L. G., 110
Birchfield, Mrs. Ezekiel, 159n
Bishop, D., 67
    William, 146n
Blackburn, Robert, 51
Blackmore, Nathaniel, 51
Blair, John, 29
Blevins, Robert, 146n
Blount, Wm. 27
Boone, Daniel, 2
    John, 9
Boring, Mrs. J. R. 157n
Bowers, Daniel S., 146n
    David, 91n
    J. L., 91n
    John T., 146n
    Leonard, 76n 81, 83, 87
    R. B., 91n
    Valentine, 91, 94, 152
    William C., 96n 99n
Boyd, William, 87, 151
Bradley, James L. 40, 54n 167n 168n
Brewer, Benjamin, 111, 113, 115n
    Mrs. Sallie Stewart, 155
Brian, Nancy, 80
Brooks, Reuben, 163, 169n
Brown, George, 135
    Isacc H., 69, 91n
    Jacob, 8n, 12n, 14n
    John, 33n, 75n, 87
    Joseph, 31

Brownlow, William G., 55-59, 65, 68-70, 103-104, 107, 129-130, 170, 165
Broyles, Matthias, 84
Buck, David, 67
    Elijah, 83
    Jonathan 76n, 83
    Nathaniel, 142n
Burrow, James, 53n, 109
Burts, Joseph S., 39

Cameron, Alexander, 6, 14
    Jacob, 67, 112, 115n, 127 134, 157, 108
    Dr. James M., 53n, 116
    Jane, 157
    John W., 166
    Margaret, 109n
Campbell, Arthur, 22
    Elisha, 94
    Isaac, 81
    J. B., 93n
    Jeremiah, 38, 46n, 49
    Joe, 102
    "Uncle John", 123n
    Josiah, 37
    Riley, 122
    Smith, 67
    Solomon, 35n
    W. G., 94
    Col. William, 17, 18
    Zachariah, 32, 34, 50
Cannon, Jeremiah, 146n
    Gov. Newton, 49, 56n
Carr, Alfred, 85n
    Richard, 82
Carriger, Christian E., 39n, 47n, 49, 66n, 154
    Godfrey, Jr., 35n, 146
    Godfrey, Sr., 149, 151-153
    John, 67, 152
    Captain Nicholas, 149n
Carter, Alfred M., 38, 51, 54n, 69 110, 111, 113, 115n, 126 152, 153, 155
    Edy, (col.) 155, 160
    Elizabeth, McLin, 32, 155, 160
    Elizabeth, Sr., 115n
    Emily P., 114
    David, W., 67, 112, 127
    Mrs. Eva, 116n
    James P. T., 67, 167

Carter, John, 8-10, 13-16, 21, 30, 32n, 33, 151
   Landon, 20n, 21, 24, 28, 30, 32-34, 50, 110, 124, 149-151, 155, 167n, 170
   Landon D., 114
   Lamuel P., 66n
   William B., 38, 47n, 51, 56n, 67, 117, 126, 129, 152, 153, 167n
Cass, Robert, 67n
Cass, James F., 142n
Cate, William, 94, 96
Chambers, James, 75n, 76
Chastain, Charles, 73n
   John, 73n
Christian, Col. William, 15
Clark, Josiah, 151
Cleveland, Col, 18
Cobb, Pharoah, 17, 149-151
Coffin, Dr. Charles, 110
Cole, Benjamin, 67, 90
   Israel, 146n
Collins, G. O., 143
   John, 102
   Katie, 143
Colyer, Charles, 35
Conner, Julius, 151
Cooke, John, 154
Cooper, J., 67
Cooper, Joe, 75n
   Joel, 145
Cornwallis, Lord, 19, 18
Cox, Abraham, 151
   Caleb, 67
   Caleb B., 146n
Crawford, W., 115n
Crouch, J. M., 98
   Jonathan, 96n
   Joseph, 81, 83
Crowe, Christian, 169n
Crutcher, W. J., 167n
Cunningham, Aaron, 35
   J. W. 114
   John F., 113
   William, 51
Curtis, John, 122
Cutbirth, Benjamin, Sr., 151

Daily, Catherine, 109n
   Elizabeth, 109n
   Hiram, 104, 108
   Nancy A., 109n
   Wm. C., 109n

Daniel, Wm., 75n
Davis, Amos, 49n
   Wm., 87, 151
Dean, William, 66n
Doak, Rev. Samuel, 18, 20, 109
Dodge, Jereil, 80, 81, 118
Doran, Alexander, 36n, 37, 46n, 125, 156
Donelson, John, 6, 20
Dorrell, Wm. T., 107
Drake, Henry 51
Duffield, George, 51, 125, 126n, 156, 171, 193-194
   H. C., 126n
Dugger, Julius Caesar, 3, 101
   William, 35n
   Jules, 35n
   John, 84
Duncan, Jeremiah, 31, 149n
Dunlap, John, 81

Edens, James, 10, 76n, 79, 80, 83, 84, 85n, 92, 94
   James, Sr., 151
Ellis, Dan, Capt., 6n, 109, 102n
   "Uncle Grant," 6n
   Radford, 121-123
Elrod, Callaway, 168n
Embree, Elihue, 153
Emmert, Abraham, 97
   Andrew, 146n
   George, 33n, 49, 67, 97, 99n, 145
   J., 167n
   Peter, 107, 121, 134
   W. C., 169n
English, Samuel, 153
Ensor, Thomas P., 53n, 67, 97, 99n
   David J., 53n
Even, Thomas, 79, 88-89

Ferguson, Major Patrick, 17-19
Fisk, Stephen, 128, 130
Fitzsimmons, Millard, Jr., 59n
   Millard, Sr., 59n
   W. R., 53, 59
Flemming, Wm. M., 39
Fletcher, Eli, 142n
Folsom, Major H. M., 158n, 163, 169n
   G. W. 109n
   Malcolm N., 40, 67, 134n
   Nathaniel 33-35
Forbes, Simeon, 67n, 107
Ford, Joseph 35n, 149n
Franklin, Benjamin, 23
Fulkerson, Abraham, 99n
Fulton, D. T., 103

Furman, Wood, 128-129
    Mrs. Wood, 129n, 132n, 133

Garland, Guttredge, 34
    Valentine 58, 59
Gifford, J. P. T., 93n
Gott, William 45n, 55, 112-115n,
    127, 132, 143
Gourley, Thomas 49, 145n
    James 119, 120
Graham, Wm., 126
Greer, Alexander, 36n, 37, 151
    Andrew, 3, 16n, 34, 36n, 50, 76n,
    100
    Andrew, Sr., 32, 48n, 149, 151
    John, 125
    Mary, 152
Griffin, Wm. 151
Grindstaff, Ezekiel 49n
    Michael, 67, 123

Hail, Meshek, 73, 75n, 148n
Haines, George, 31
Hall, Alexander, 120
    " Uncle Lide" 123n
Hammer, John 87
Hammitt, Rebekah, 80
Hampton, Johnson, 38, 46n
    Johnston, 152
    Lawson W., 39n, 67
Handley, Samuel 28
Harden, Elijah D. 95, 96
    John N. 67n
Hardin, E. D. 91n
    W. N. 146n
Harkleroad, Daniel 33n
Harris, A. N. 105
Hart, Leonard 10
Hatcher, William 84, 85n
Hathaway, John 92, 96
    Jonathan 91n
Hayne, Robert Y. 63
Haynes, Landon C. 163, 166
Head, Alexander 90n
Heiskell, Joseph B. 168
Henderson, Judge Richard 11, 12n
Hendrickson, J. 167n
Hendrix, John 122
    Molly 82
    Solomon 76, 78, 79, 82, 85n, 87
Henry, Abraham 51, 125
    Edward, 82
Hickey, James 167

Hill, John 123
Hilton, T. M. 167n
Hinkle, Fred 73n, 77n 87n
Hiter, William 78
Hoffmeister, J. M. 115, 116
Holly, David 122
Honeycut, John 3
Houghton, Joshua 10, 12n, 148n
    Joshua, Jr. 148n
    Thomas, 10, 16n, 148n
Hover, Mrs. 131, 135
Howard, Caroline 135
    Ira 119
    Isaac 135n
    Moriah 158n
Huffman, Ann E. 114
    Elizabeth 114
    William 95
Humfrey, Jessee 156
    Mary 156n
    Molly 82
Hunt, Uriah 78
Hyder, J. E. 93
    J. Hampton (Uncle Hampie)
    73n, 84, 92, 97
    J. N. 93n
    J. O. L. 93n
    James 142n
    Jesse 93n
    John H. 66n
    Michael, 10, 119n
    Michael, Jr., 35n
    Michael E. 119
    Sam 119n

Ireland, James 73n
Isbell, Zachariah 8, 14n

Jackson, A. E. 166
Jenkins, Jessee 136
    Larkin 136
    Rowland, 51, 136
    Sanford, 169n
    William, 136
Jobe, Dr. Abraham 158, 161, 168, 169
    David, 73
    John 53n, 66n
    Wm. 84
    Wm. (col.) 160
Johnson, Thomas 43-47
    Thomas C. 95, 97, 99n
    James 51
    James S. 51, 152
    Mary Ann 102n

Jones, James 80
    John 14n
    William D. 108n, 111
    Willie, 16
Julian, James N, 65n
    Pierce 65n

Keener, D. 67
Kelly, Joshua 73, 75n, 76
Keys, James 38, 49
King, J. R. 111
Kite, Granville 94
Kitzmiller, Martin V. 96, 98
Kuhn, Peter 76n, 84

Lackey, Thomas, 33n
Lacy, Alexander, 67
    J. C., 67
    Jack, 122
    James, 33n, 79
    James W., 67
    John, 94
    Mark, 97, 99n
"Lallow, Cit" (col.) 156 (Doran)
Lambert, Jeremiah, 21, 100
Lands, Joseph, 34, 35n
Lane, Tidence, 72, 73n 77
Lewis, J. G., 167n
    Lewis D., 67n
    William, 94
Lile, Henry, 148n
Lincoln, Isaac, 149, 151, 153
    Mary, 153
Lipps, Jonathan, 67, 79, 89, 90, 90n
Little, Henry 122
Livingston, J. W., 92
Long, W. R., 106
Love, Robert, 66n, 68, 169n
    Thomas D., 152
Loves, The, 87
Lucas, Robert, 14n, 21, 148n
    William, 115n
Lusk, Alexander, S. Y. 142n
    Robert, 35n
    Tennessee H., 142n
Lyle, John, 39
    Henry, 10
Lyon, Mason R., 55, 57, 58, 84, 94-96
    130
    W. C., 91n.

MacLin, John, 35n
    William 30n, 148n
Magee, Dr., 116

Marsh, William, 167n
Marshall, L. G. 103
Mason, Joseph, 33n
May, Joh, 102
McAllister, John 153
McDowell, Col. Charles, 18
McInturff, Thomas, 67
McKay, Jeremiah, 73n
McLin, James, 111, 114, 128, 130
McNabb, David, 32, 34, 36n, 50
    Elly, 82
    John, 16n
    Taylor, 49
McNabbs, the, 87
Millard, S. H., 123
Miller, Jacob, 33n
    James, 80, 82, 118, 120
    Nancy, 80
    Samuel, 142n
Miner, John, 53n
Moore, Albert, 139n
Morris, Gideon, 148n
Morton, Alexander F., 94
Mottern, George, 122
    "Uncle George" 122n
    "Aunt Julie" 122n
    Susana, 122
    Tilda, 122
Mulkey, Jonathan, 72, 73n, 76, 78, 79, 85n
    Philip, Jr., 72
    Philip, Sr., 72
Murrel, Richard, 83
Musgrove, Samuel, 35

Nave, Christian C., 146n
    David, 146n
    Godfrey, 39n, 67, 152
    Isaac L., 169n
    J. D., 91n
    J. T. B., 91n
    Jacob, 169n
    John, 46n, 81, 91n, 146n
    Henry, 84, 85n, 91n, 146n, 169n
    Levi, 146n
    Teeter, 10
Nelson, Carrick W., 39n, 40n, 52n.
    54n, 64, 66n, 67, 115n
    David, 50, 52n, 54n, 64, 67,
    108n, 112, 114, 139
    Jacob, B., 136
    James W., 58
    M. W., 54n, 64
    Mary, 109n
    Phoebe, 109n

Nelson, Thomas A. R., 51, 52n, 63
    64, 66, 70, 138, 139n, 162, 164
    166, 168
Nethy, Joseph, 155n
Newell, William C., 96n
Noble, David W., 37

O,Brien, Eliza Ann, 103
    J., 108n
    James, 45n, 103n
    Joel S., 49n
    Joseph, Sr., 67
    M. G., 167n
O'Briens, 109, 155n
Odle, Abraham, 76n
Otis, Ashbell, 111
Owens, Owen, 74

Patterson, Gowen, 153
    John, 153
Patton, Mrs. Bob, 159n
    Mary, 17
    S. D., 67
Pearce, A. K., 91n
Pearson, Abel, 33n
Peoples, Alfred, 49n
    Dianah, (col.) 162
    George W., 157n
    John, 35n, 151
Perkins, Susana, 80
Perry, J., 167n
Poindexter, James, 81
Poland, John, 35n
Polin, John, 87
Potter, John, 149
Powell Joseph, 43, 44, 45n, 52n, 96,134n
    Samuel, 47
    Thomas J., 53n
Price, James, 134n
Pugh, David, 82, 85n
    Jonathan, 67
Pughs, 87

Randolph, William, 74
Range, Alfred, 122
    E. H., 85n, 95n
    Elkanah, 122
    Harrison, 122
    Henry, 122
    Jake, 122
    James, 35n
    Jim, 122

Reasoner, Garret, 149n
Reeve, C., 67
    Clayton, 157n
    Robert, 45n
Reeves, William, 4n, 109n
Redman, Stephen, 35n
Reneau, John, 33n
Renfro, Fanny, 80-82, 118, 161 (col)?
Renfro, John, 99n
    Joseph, 82
Reno, Charles, 51
    William, 77n
Rhea, John, 47
    William R., 112, 113, 115n
Rich, William, 115n
Robertson, Ann, 15n
    Charles, 8
    Charles, 4n, 12, 14n, 16n, 20,
    28, 73n
    Henderson, 109, 132
    James, 3, 4, 8, 9, 14n, 15, 16, 20, 67n
    John, 35n
    Jonathan, 4n
    Mark, 4n
Robertsons, The, 9, 10
Rockhold, W. W., 53n
Roiston, Joshua, 33n
Russell, George, 14n
Ryan, George W., 102n, 109n

Sandford, Robert, 78
Satterfield, P. Q., 128n
Sawyer, S., 111
Scott, James, 109n
    Samuel W., 167n
Sevier, John, 8n, 10, 14n, 15, 16,
    18-20, 23-27, 30n
    Valentine, 10
Shelby, Captain Evan, Jr., 15
    Colonel Evan, 17-19
Sherfy, Solomon Q., 128n
Sherrill, Catherine (Bonny Kate), 15n
Shipley, Nathan, 81
Simpson, James C., 112
Singletary, Elizabeth C., 131, 143n
    John, 53n, 58, 102, 104, 107-109
    V., 167n
Slagle, H., 167n——Slagle, L., 167n
Smith, Daniel, 154
    Elisha, 67
    George, 128
    H. C., 167n

Smith, Hamilton C., 66n--Henry, 111
    Jack, 116
    Jacob, 154
    James, 12, 14n
    John M., 167n
    "Aunt Nannie" 143n
    Nicholas, 80
    William Bailey, 12
    William W., 67, 107
Smyth, E., John, 155n
Snapp, Jacob K., 54n
Snyder, J., 122
Solomon, 122n; --W. M., 123
Spurgin, E., 96n
Stout, D., 67
Stover, Daniel, 85n, 91n, 165, 166, 167n
    Mrs. Daniel, 165n
    David L., 66n, 79, 146
    S. M., 116
    Sol, 91n
    William, 96, 169n
Stuart, Henry, 14
    James, 28, 29, 148n
    Robert, 148n
Sullivan, Gen. John, 16
Swingle, L. M., 58

Talbot, Agnes, 7, 73
    Matthew, 17, 72, 73n, 148n
    Thomas, 24
Talbots, the 87
Tatham, William 14n, 15
Taylor, A. W. 56n, 129n, 134, 155, 156, 158n, 169n
    Alf, 107
    Andrew, 10, 36n, 37, 46, 125n, 149
    "Aunt Jo" (col.), 153n, 154n, 158n 159
    Bob, 159
    George, 153n
    Isaac, 87
    James P., Col., 44, 45, 107, 126, 152, 153
    John, 146n
    Leroy, 28
    M. C., 115n
    Mary, 107, 115n
    N. G., 66n, 67, 70, 107-109 134n, 163, 164, 166
    N. M., 169n
    Nathaniel, 31, 34, 35n, 125, 149n, 150, 151, 153, 155n
    Tina, (col), 153n, 154n, 158n
    W., 93n
    William, 69n, 153n
  Temple, Oliver P., 68

Tipton, A., 167n
    Abraham, 33n, 40, 54, 66n, 95-97, 99n, 166
    Albert J., 39n, 102, 104
    Isaac P., 49, 67
    James I., 120, 121, 123, 126, 128 134, 145n, 153, 162
    John, 24, 28, 29, 30n, 32n
    Jonathan, Fr., 31, 151
    Joseph, 87, 151
    Samuel, 12n, 32n, 33, 35, 51, 73n, 76n, 78, 81, 151
    Samuel, Jr., 93n, 94
    "Aunt Mary Bob" (col.) 162
Thomas, A., 159n
Thompkins, Joseph, 36n
Thornton, Rhueben, 32, 34, 36n, 37, 46n, 51, 125n, 149n
Toncray, Charles P., 166, 167n
Toncrays, the, 109
Trace, Timothy, 73

Underwood, Richard 67

Vandeventer, Jacob 67n
Van Huss, J. P. 91n
    Matthais 146n
Vaught, John 34, 36n
    Joseph 152
Vest, Solomon 122

Walker, Ben 145
    Felix, 14n
    "Uncle Joe" 145
    Nancy 145
Wagner, David 149, 151
Wall, Wm. 74
Watson, Samuel 51
Wayne, Gen. Anthony 24, 24n
Wells, R. P. 111
White, Benjamin 81, 90n, 139n, 146n
    James 85n
    Hugh 36n
    Judge Hugh 164
    Lawson 49
    Richard C., 39n, 67, 150, 151
Whitehead, John 81
    Sarah 80
Whitson, Jesse 151
    Thomas 35n
Wilcox, C. 167n
    D. P. 102n
    M. F. 109n
Williams, Archibald 36n, 151
    Edmond, Jr. 40n, 87
    Edmond, Sr. 28, 148n, 149
    George 35n, 46, 125, 151

Williams, George "Dot" 145
    John 46n
    John L. 139n
    John S. 46n
    Joshua 10
    Lucretia 151
    Mordecai 146n
    Pleasant 91n
    Robert 167n
    Samuel W. 43, 44, 66n, 67
    Judge Samuel C. 73
    William 66n
Willis, Henry 100
Wilson, J. D. 111
Wilson, L. L. 67
Witt, Caleb 81
Womack, Jacob 14n, 16
Worley, John 35n
Wright, David 120, 123
    George, 145
    John 39n, 118, 120-121
    Thomas 121, 123

CPSIA information can be obtained
at www.ICGtesting.com
Printed in the USA
BVOW11s1649151117
500481BV00004B/526/P